THE GOD OF SECOND CHANCES

THE GOD OF SECOND CHANCES

DON BAKER

VICTOR BOOKS®

A DIVISION OF SCRIPTURE PRESS PUBLICATIONS INC.
USA CANADA ENGLAND

Scripture quotations are from *New American Standard Bible,* © the
Lockman Foundation 1960, 1962, 1963, 1968, 1971, 1972, 1973, 1975, 1977.

Library of Congress Cataloging-in-Publication Data

Baker, Don.
   The God of second chances / Don Baker.
     p   cm.
   Includes bibliographical references.
   ISBN 0-89693-000-9
   1. Moses (Biblical leader) — Meditations.   2. Trust in God.
   I. Title.
   BS580.M6B24   1991
   222'.1092 — dc20   90-24354
                                  CIP

1 2 3 4 5 6 7 8 9 10 Printing/Year 95 94 93 92 91

**To my father, Harry,
and my mother, Helen,
who gave me my first look at God
and lovingly introduced their son
to His Son.**

PREFACE

If there is anything we need during life's baffling and bewildering experiences, it is not an explanation, but a trust in *the God of second chances*.

To be dropped from earth's highest human pinnacle through the clouds of fame and glory onto the burning sands of the world's wasteland was to Moses a baffling and bewildering experience. For forty interminable years, the pharaoh-elect of the glorious and powerful kingdom of Egypt was forced to lead a life of obscurity in a land that he hated, performing a job that, to an Egyptian, was the most demeaning task on earth.

It was during this baffling, bewildering experience that Moses met God, beheld His glory, and became His friend.

To have a "friend of God" available to trace God's image in clear and unmistakable word pictures is a special privilege. Moses knew God—loved God—obeyed God—talked with God, and actually caught a brief glimpse of God. He spent enough time in God's presence to even absorb some of His resplendent glory and then display it to others.

Moses knew God. But as I began to learn some lessons from him, I realized that I not only wanted to know more about God, I also needed to know more about Moses.

Moses lived for 120 years, yet the Scriptures describe only one-third of his lifetime. Like Jesus, we have record of his birth, but only brief sketches of his first forty years in Egypt. We do know from the Bible that he was saved from death in the Nile by the princess to the pharaoh. In history she remains unnamed. It is possible that she was Hatshepsut, who later reigned as queen over Egypt.

With many Old Testament scholars I have assumed that Moses, by virtue of his adoptive relationship, was heir to the throne of Egypt even though he was born a Hebrew.

I have also assumed that Jochebed, his Hebrew mother, was unable to teach enough about his Hebrew heritage in the first two to three years of his life to prevent him from becoming an idolater during his time in the palace, and that he became familiar with all the ways of the Egyptians, which would include their polytheistic religion.

Very little detailed information is available on the period of time spent in Midian, the second forty-year period of his life.

To reach back in history 3,500 years and "flesh out" a man, his contemporaries, and his culture became a difficult but exciting adventure.

My search for information was sparked by innocent questions that displayed some terribly wide gaps in my learning. My own chronological ignorance was exposed when people asked, "Did the Hebrew slaves build the pyramids of Egypt?" Or, "Were the pyramids in existence when Moses lived?" Or, "Who was Egypt's pharaoh when Moses was growing up in the palace?"

Egyptian records give only fleeting glimpses of the Hebrew slavery, and no mention of Moses. I did find bas-reliefs of Hebrews in chains in Luxor at the Temple of Karnak, and was shown one line from Merneptah's famous stele in the Cairo Museum which reads, "The people of Israel is desolate, it has no offspring." Other than that, the land of the Nile is silent.

For other information, it became necessary to exhaust the contents of numerous books, to interview historians, to search the ruins of an ancient civilization, to walk through the great and terrible wilderness of Sinai, and eventually to climb to the peak of Jebel Musa— "the mountain of Moses," one of the world's most forbidding mountains—in an attempt to see and feel what Moses experienced in his historic encounter with God.

One conclusion after all of the studying and traveling was that a knowledge of ancient Egypt can be tremendously helpful to the student of the Bible in helping one to understand much of the Old Testament.

Norris and Margaret Aldeen, my wife Martha and I, spent long, hot, tiring days and nights on foot, in cars, on the backs of camels, and in feluccas and barges on the Nile in search of anything that would shed some light on a vague and obscure period of time in human history. We even tried to set fire to an acacia tree that stood alone in that vast desert.

For years it was generally accepted that the oppression and the Exodus occurred during the Nineteenth Dynasty under such kings as Rameses I and Seti II and Rameses II sometime between 1319 and 1237 B.C. This posed a chronological dilemma when we date the fall of the City of Jericho nearly one hundred years before the birth of any of those kings.

More recent scholarship places Moses in Egypt during the reigns of Thutmose III and Amenhotep II (1490-1425 B.C.). These two were among Egypt's grandest pharaohs and led their nation into the age of its greatest glory.

As for the pyramids, they were not only seen by Moses, but also by Abraham and Joseph. They had been erected a thousand years before baby Moses took his first boat trip down the Nile. They were as visible to Moses 3,500 years ago as they were to me this past year as I looked west from the top floor of Cairo's Nile Hilton Hotel.

The Hebrews built cities and canals and walls and towers, but they built no pyramids. Most of the labor force of thousands came from the Egyptians in the off-season when the farmlands were flooded and the farmers were idle.

Did Moses know Job? The suggestion that they may have met is mere conjecture. The dating and the authorship of Job, which may well have been the first book of the Bible to be written, is unknown. Job quite possibly lived during Moses' time and probably in a nearby country.

Literary license? Of course I've taken literary license, and described feelings and happenings that are not documented. I have, however, found nearly every incident recorded in this book mentioned or alluded to elsewhere. I must admit, though, that some were discovered only in the hidden regions of my own imagination.

To couch truth in narrative form is difficult and sometimes dangerous, since it requires a strange mixing of fact with fiction.

The biblical data remain intact. The dialogue between God and Moses is just as it is recorded in Scripture. The self-revelation of God unfolds in the same manner as it was unfolded to Moses. The greatest weakness is my own inadequacy when it comes to comprehending and revealing the infinite majesty, the incomprehensible glory, and the limitless wonder of Jehovah God.

My deep gratitude is extended to my church family who permitted the time to travel and write, to the Aldeens who accompanied us, to scholars like Dr. Ralph Alexander of Western Conservative Baptist Seminary, Mr. Jim Monson of the Institute of Holy Land Studies, Dr. Gleason Archer of Trinity Evangelical Divinity School, and to Emil in Luxor, and Omima, Muhamed, and Abdu in Cairo and Sinai, and to Richard in Israel, who assisted us in our search.

For Moses, banished to the wilderness of Midian, life had stopped completely and permanently.

CHAPTER ONE

(Exodus 3:1

"Now Moses was pasturing the flock of Jethro. . . ." (Exodus 3:1).

Moses picked up a smooth stone and hurled it beyond the feet of a straying goat. The animal leaped in surprise and then wandered meekly back in the direction of his shepherd.

A new day had just begun—another in the endless succession of days that comprised the meaningless existence of a prince who had turned into a shepherd.

For Moses, banished to the desert wilderness of Midian, life had stopped completely and permanently.

His days dragged on endlessly.

They had become days without meaning—days without purpose.

From the moment the early morning sun rose above the tips of nearby peaks and sprang up into the clear, cloudless sky until it sank into the purple shroud that lay along the west, time was endless.

Each day was the same.

Each moment was a repetition of the meaningless, purposeless moments that had just preceded it.

The hours passed into days.

The days into weeks.

The weeks into months.

The months into years—forty of them.

Forty interminable years sentenced to the solitude and obscurity and pain of a pointless existence. Sentenced to nothingness.

Forty years leading stupid, irascible, worthless animals across the burning sands of an endless desert when he could have been leading the world's greatest empire into realms of eternal glory.

That great and terrible wilderness called Sinai—the triangular-shaped peninsula that links Africa to Asia, noted for its barrenness and desolation and its vast expanses of desert broken only by jagged peaks—had become his prison.

The sky had begun to brighten from the deep blue of the night to an early morning white as the sun began its long climb from behind the distant mountains.

The moon was riding high overhead.

The morning star was still visible.

The ranging peaks that nearly surrounded the immense bowl-shaped plain stretching out before him took on the appearance of brilliant flames. Flames that danced heavenward as the individual rays of the rising sun began to strike the tops of the stark, red granite peaks.

A covey of quail flew low over the restless flock of sheep and goats. A hawk cried in the distance. Other than that lone, plaintive sound, the earth was still.

The morning sun's climb was long and arduous before it finally reached high enough to appear as a magnificent halo of light on top of the distant peaks.

Its appearance brought immediate relief from the night's chill. Its brilliance illuminated an awesome, foreboding, even frightening range of bare mountains— scarred and seamed—that raised their heads high into the azure sky. An immense mass of mountains existing for no discernible purpose.

They mark no boundary between nations.

They possess no vast treasure of mineral or metal.

They contain no vegetation.

They collect only little water to irrigate the desert plain beneath them.

They comprise only immense slabs of stone—vast accumulations of rock and sand with boulders the size of buildings strewn from top to bottom.

Each time he moved toward this awesome range of magnificent mountains, Moses was reminded of another life, another time. Another world.

The perpendicular peaks caused him to remember the great buildings of a distant land. In them he could see columns and pylons and obelisks. Even an occasional pyramid would take shape as the sun's shadows moved slowly across the changing face of a range called Horeb.

His memory stirred. His mind drifted back to a glorious existence that lasted for years but ended in only a day. Just one day in life's long procession of time. One day that completely extinguished the glory—and left only ashes behind.

The striking figure of the prince was no less commanding than the grand objects in the distance. It seemed that all the gods of Egypt had set their seal upon him.

CHAPTER TWO

(Exodus 2:1-14)

"Moses . . . was a man of power in words and deeds" (Acts 7:22).

The day that haunted Moses' memory had begun like any other day in the life of the prince.

The eastern sky had the appearance of sapphire blended with gold dust. The yet invisible sun cast a fan of pale orange radiance heavenward in advance of its journey across the cloudless heavens that blanketed the land of the ancient pharaohs.

As night withdrew, the royal son of Egypt, the prince of earth's greatest empire—the pharaoh-elect—stood as he did every morning, waiting for the god of the day to roll up into view and cast its luminescent beams upon the splendor that had long been called the "Garden of the World."

From the terrace of his luxurious royal apartment he saw the first finger of early morning brilliance reach across the brightening sky and lightly touch the glistening tips of a row of majestic mountains—man-made mountains that had been hewn from solid stone.

The thousand-year-old pyramids of Giza, cased in white limestone and polished to a mirror-like finish, had lost none of their shining grandeur in the first millennium of their existence.

The stately prince, now in his thirty-ninth year, flicked a fly from his face and marveled afresh at the glitter of the structures that towered in the pure desert air.

Under the dancing rays of the rising sun, they took on the appearance of gigantic prisms strategically placed in the ever-drifting sands.

He rehearsed again the well-known tales of their architect, Amhotep, who some said was a god who became a man and descended to the Valley of the Nile for no other reason than to design and construct these massive mausoleums as eternal apartment houses for Egypt's dead kings.

The symmetry of the pyramids was identical and perfect. Each of their finely honed sides sloped at the same precise trigonometric angle of slightly more than fifty-one degrees.

The striking figure of the prince was no less commanding than the grand objects in the distance. It seemed that all the gods of Egypt had set their seal upon him.

Every graceful movement of his person, his rich and resonant voice, his lordly eyes, his superb height and magnificent carriage combined to speak of a man born to rule—a man created for dominion over men.

Upon his head of carefully trimmed jet-black hair, he placed a rich cap of green silk, the front of which was shaped like a hawk, the symbol of Horus. The eyes of the hawk blazed with diamonds. Its plumage was studded with precious stones of beryl and onyx.

From behind the cap a short cape fell over his broad shoulders like drooping wings.

His jacket was of fine linen embroidered with gold. It opened in front, displaying a broad belt of links of steel and gold exquisitely and cunningly woven together.

About his neck hung a collar of red-hued gold.

His broad, manly chest was covered by a breastplate of defensive armor. On its center sparkled an emerald nameplate—a cartouche—bearing in hieroglyphics the name of MOSES, Egypt's future king.

As he buckled on his jeweled sword and placed on his head a close-fitting helmet of burnished gold, he took on the appearance of an Egyptian god of war.

He took one last glance at the west. The pyramids now bathed in the splendor of the morning sun.

Even the sphinx with its body of a lion and its head of a man, guarding the great pyramid of Cheops, was visible.

The Nile—the eternal, muddy Nile—the very life of Egypt that flowed from the heart of equatorial Africa to the Mediterranean, was already teeming with life.

Eagles from the delta soared overhead.

Snow-white birds with black-tipped wings skimmed the tops of the waves. A crocodile slithered from the river bank, slipped its ugly body beneath the waves and began silently gliding its fearsome hulk in search of an early morning breakfast.

The prince, with his ever-present fly flail in hand, again flicked the pests from his head, saluted the new day, and walked down the highly polished tile steps. He strode past the lush green foliage of his spacious court-yard to his waiting chariot, completely unaware that before the sun finished this day's journey across the sky his world would completely end.

His reign as Egypt's prince would be finished.

The future king of the world's greatest and oldest empire would be nothing more than a dim memory in the minds of only a few.

Not only was Moses Egypt's military commander, but as prince and successor to the pharaoh he was acknowledged to be the first priest of the realm, destined upon his succession to the throne to become a god.

CHAPTER THREE

(Exodus 2:1-14)

"Moses was educated in all the learning of the Egyptians. . . ." (Acts 7:22).

Years of disciplined training had prepared Moses for this new day.

As the adopted son of Egypt's king, he had been schooled in the Harvard of the ancient world—the temple of the Sun—the empire's highest place of higher learning.

He had studied

the sciences
mathematics
astronomy
chemistry
medicine
philosophy and law,

until he had mastered each.

He had been trained in

the arts
music
sculpture and painting,

until he possessed the broadest knowledge of all.

Moses was an author. He could masterfully write exciting stories of military conquests and historical sagas on papyrus or in cuneiform on tablets.

He was taught the protocol of kings and trained in all the martial arts of a nation that in the most recent centuries had entertained thoughts of world domination.

Fifteen hundred years of Egypt's existence were already history. He knew it well. He could list the rulers and their exploits through the eighteen dynasties that preceded him.

He knew the secret of the pyramids.

The prince of Egypt had become adept in the use of the spear, the javelin, and the sword.

He was skilled in all the light and heavy artillery of the ancient world. He was a master charioteer. Often he would lead Egypt's magnificent divisions of four thousand chariots on proud display before his king. As he leaped on his war chariot inlaid with silver and gold and protected only in front with a curved shield, the Ethiopian slaves who held the reins would leap aside. The horses would then spring to life and race down the runway until Moses reached his position of command. He would perform an abrupt stop, lift his right arm high in the air, and then lead his waiting charioteers, 100 abreast, in full military review. The ground would literally shake under the roll of eight thousand wheels and twice as many horses' hooves.

Moses, from his youth, learned endurance and developed stamina by running twenty-two miles each day.

He became a great military leader. As general of the armies of Egypt he would often accompany his king on missions of conquest to Kadesh, Megiddo, Salem, and Damascus.

His armies had passed through the valley to the east of Megiddo—later known as Armageddon—in plain view of the destined hometown of Jesus, whose birth was still fourteen centuries in the future.

In the early days of Egypt's new kingdom, the domination of this expanding empire was extended to the very shores of the great river Euphrates.

At the head of the nation's growing military might, Moses marched beyond the gates of Thebes to engage Occhoris of Ethiopia in a seesaw battle that finally ended in total victory. No news of battle brought greater joy than that of the fall of their longtime enemy.

Moses' triumphant return to Memphis, leading his defeated foe captive at the wheels of his chariot, won the adoration of the empire.

Not only was Moses Egypt's military commander, but as prince and successor to the pharaoh he was acknowledged to be the first priest of the realm, destined upon his succession to the throne to become a god.

Egypt was the land of many gods, and Moses knew them well and worshiped them devoutly.

The city of the Sun, near Memphis, contained 360 dazzling temples for 360 separate deities—one for each day of the Egyptian calendar year.

Each community had its resident god.

Each Egyptian had his own personal god.

The pharaoh was a god. He was the chief unifying factor in Egyptian religious life—the chief priest in every temple. He was the only person besides the high priest who was qualified to officiate in the most sacred temple of rituals—the only one permitted to enter their holy of holies.

As the titular son of Re, the sun-god, he was both human and divine. His duty was to make certain that Egypt continued functioning.

He made the sun to rise and to set.

He made the Nile to flood and to ebb.

He caused the grain to grow.

Each year, Moses would board his royal barge for his annual pilgrimage south to the upper Nile, disembarking at the splendid city of Thebes. In reverent silence he would study the tombs of the kings to the west, and the temples of Karnak and Luxor to the east. With practiced solemnity he would walk through the western gate of Karnak, the most massive of all the ancient temples, down the avenue of ram-headed sphinxes, and through the sanctuary to the sacred lake of purification and pool of the crocodiles.

As he entered the outer court, he would be surrounded by great pylon gates and lofty obelisks. Passing through ornate vestibules and chambers, he would gaze up at mighty colonnades covered with bas-reliefs and hieroglyphs—each seeming to rise to the very heavens.

He was forbidden entrance to only one room, the holy place where Amun—the cosmic creator-god, self-existent and self-engendered—resided.

Amun was believed to have no father and no mother. He shaped his egg and mingled his own seed to make himself come into being. He gave birth to all the gods. He separated earth from the heavens. From Thebes he created the whole universe.

Moses visited all the temples of all the gods. He left his gifts at their altars.

He worshiped Apis the bull—a bull-calf honored for his great strength, and mummified at his death.

He worshiped Aten Re, the god of the sun disk; Shu, the god of the light; and Nut, the sky goddess who held up the heavens.

He could name all the gods—Atum and Re and Khepri and Isis and Horus. He knew all about Osiris, the god of death, who was killed and brought back to life to become the lord and judge over the realm of the dead. Moses understood all the elaborate preparations for a future life that had become the prime concern of every Egyptian as he faced the prospect of judgment followed by an eternity in paradise or in hell.

The figures of the gods were hewn in marble, in granite, and in sandstone or diorite, and were fashioned in the various forms established by long tradition.

One would appear in the form of a man joined to the head of a falcon. Another as a bird with the head of a man. Others with the head of a dog or a hawk or a crocodile. One was in the shape of a beetle.

Moses knew all about the rituals of worship. He knew how to rouse these gods to action, how to pacify them, and how to appease them. He knew how to use them to best advantage in a kingdom that depended upon its incantations and its rituals to sustain its life.

He knew all the myths about their private lives. The legends of ancient Egypt spared none of the scandalous details when they spoke of their gods. Tales of rape, incest, and murder were common as the gods jockeyed for power.

The one God Moses didn't know was the God of the Hebrews, the resident slaves of Egypt. A nation of prisoners. In 350 years they had grown from just one family to a people numbering nearly two million.

Through his mother's early training he knew about this God. He marveled that just one God could oversee all the details of the universe and still satisfy the needs of man. Moses felt an instinctive tug from somewhere deep within whenever he heard His name.

All of Egypt's gods were related to *things;* the god of the sun, the god of the Nile, the god of war, the god of the heavens, and the god of the crops. The Hebrew God seemed to be related to *people.* He was always referred to as the God of Abraham and the God of Isaac and the God of Jacob. He seemed to be a people-God, a personal God. Moses knew no such deity among all those worshiped in the land of Egypt.

Moses had studied the history of the Hebrews. He knew about Prince Abraham, who traveled from the east to dwell briefly in Egypt. He knew about Isaac and Jacob and about Joseph, the man who had saved the country during the time of its great famine. He had seen the remains of the granaries built by this Hebrew who had displayed such wisdom and courage.

The ancestral customs of the Hebrews were also well-known to Moses: the offering of sacrificial animals, and the rite of circumcision for all male babies at infancy—so different from Egypt, where boys were not circumcised until they neared the age of puberty.

A holy day—each week—that was set aside for rest and special acts of worship was also something foreign to Moses.

On one of his military campaigns north to Damascus he had journeyed to the distant land of Uz. He had spoken with its respected prince, a man by the name of Job. The story Job told made Moses hungry to learn more of this singular God of Egypt's slaves.

Moses had begun to experience an indescribable emptiness in his repeated acts of worship to the birds and the scarabs and the snakes and the crocodiles. And that concerned him. He was also sensing an increasing jealousy from Thutmose III over his growing popularity among the people. And that concerned him too.

Could that uneasiness be linked to those disturbing new questions about Moses' own ancestry? His dying Egyptian mother—his own, he had thought—had told him the unbelievable story of a ruling that had called for the death of all male Hebrew babies. She told him of a crude woven basket nestled in one of the canals of the Nile, of bulrushes, and of an instant love between a pharaoh's daughter and a Hebrew child. A love that had been cherished and real for more than thirty-nine years.

The secret, so well kept, was almost impossible for Moses to believe—and yet, as he studied his heavy-lidded eyes, full red lips, and high-arched, eagle-like nose, he was forced to admit that he seemed to resemble likenesses of the Hebrew prince, Abraham, more than he did the house of the pharaohs.

The glamour of Egypt's throne, the growing curiosity about the God of the Hebrews, and the intense feelings of animosity that rose up within him as the unwarranted oppression of these slave people increased, caused Moses unending anxiety and mounting confusion.

He had come to the place in his own mind where he questioned his desire to rule or even to live in a land so devoted to cruelty and magic and mystery and superstition—a land that gave greater prominence to death than to life, and placed greater value on things than on people.

Moses looked to the edge of the field. In the distance he saw a young man emerge from behind a pile of stacked bricks. He was crawling on hands and knees—writhing in pain as he attempted to dodge the lacerating blows that were being brutally rained down upon his body.

CHAPTER FOUR

(Exodus 2:1-14)

". . . He saw an Egyptian beating a Hebrew. . . ." (Exodus 2:11).

Egypt's fourteen thousand villages were just coming to life when Moses climbed into his chariot and took the reins from his Nubian slaves.

He moved rapidly through the suburbs of the city, past three great pylons uniting three magnificent courtyards. He came finally to the northern gate of the city.

The towers on each side stood ninety-nine feet high and were guarded by a detachment of tall, dark-skinned Libyan soldiers. They dipped their spears in a smart salute as Egypt's prince rode by.

Standing tall and erect in his brightly decorated chariot, and surrounded by a dozen running footmen, Moses moved further north. He drove past the groves and the gardens—past the villas and the ornamental lakes where the nobles lived during the heat of the summer.

Always in the distance, glistening in the brilliance of the early morning sun, were the obelisks and the temples, the palaces of Memphis and the pyramids of Giza.

29

It was only four miles to a desolate field, some of it partly under water. Moses stopped to rest his horses and footmen.

He surveyed again the sea of sun-blackened bodies moving—constantly moving—in the distance as they performed the never-ending, muscle-wrenching, back-breaking labor of making bricks.

These were the Hebrews—hereditary slaves of the pharaoh. They were descended from Joseph and his brothers, who had been dead for hundreds of years. A nation of immigrants which had grown so large that the insecure king of Egypt had instituted desperate measures to limit their size as well as their strength.

Male sons were again being fed to the fast-flowing waters of the Nile. The boy babies provided satisfying food for the voracious appetites of the ever-present crocodiles.

Cruelty? Not to the Egyptian point of view. Just an ingenious provision to control the population. An ancient form of abortion. And, since both the River Nile and the ravenous crocodiles were considered gods, it could be considered an act of worship.

Each pharaoh was obsessed with a determination to outdo his predecessor. Thutmose III was determined that these hordes of foreigners would build more buildings, more granaries, more canals, more temples, and more treasure cities than for any other king of any other dynasty—or they would die in the attempt.

The day had become intensely hot. Shadowing clouds were rare in Egypt. The sun bore down relentlessly, unendingly upon the bare backs of the sea of human flesh that flinched with every movement.

A score of Hebrews toiled near Moses' chariot, menaced by an overseer with a whip of thongs and a long staff. As Moses watched, an old Hebrew man slumped to the ground under the combined heat of the sun and weight of the bricks. The slave immediately came under the wrath—and the slashing whip—of the overseer.

In recent months, Moses' attitude toward these suffering slaves had swung from calloused indifference to concern, pity, and finally to anger. These Hebrews were not strangers or non-people. These were people, *his* people—descendants from the same set of ancestors. This growing realization caused him to seethe within.

That very group of toiling Hebrews he now watched from his chariot might include his own brothers or sisters—or mother or father. He'd heard the names of a man named Aaron and a woman called Miriam who were possibly his own kin.

As far as Moses could see, the earth was dark with people.

Some were stooping down with mattocks, much like modern-day picks, and were grubbing out the clay.

Others were piling it in high mounds.

Still others were chopping straw to mix with the clay and bind it.

Some were treading the clay with their bare feet to soften it.

Some were placing clay into wooden molds to shape it.

Others stood by with the king's mark or seal to stamp each brick.

The strongest were employed in raising the bricks from the earth and placing them upon the shoulders of others who carried them to a flat, open space to be dried by the heat of the sun.

Some pulled bricks on sleds with yokes placed on their shoulders, while others carried the bricks on pallets on their heads.

The borders of the busy plain, where it touched the fields of stubble, were filled with women and children gathering straw.

Moses was always troubled by the silence of the Hebrews. They never sang. They never talked. They never cried out under the whips of their overseers. Egyptians sang and talked endlessly as they worked. These

strangers from the north were strangely and frighten-
ingly silent.

The only sounds were the sharp commands of the
masters, the creak of the wheels from the carts, and the
crack of the whip as it fell on the naked backs of weary
laborers.

Often they died. Their Egyptian overseers would
leave them where they fell, denying the time for burial to
steal even a moment from the day's schedule of appointed projects. The ever-present vultures took good
care of the dead bodies.

As long as Moses remained in his chariot, detached
from the hideous scene, he could handle it well. It hurt
and it angered, but he could suppress and he could
forget.

Lately, however, Moses had been stepping down
from his distant and secure little mobile platform. He had
started walking into and through the constantly moving
sea of humanity.

Up close he could see the rising red welts from the
lash that had found its way to the backs and the shoulders of the sufferers.

He would move in closer to see them as young boys
and young girls and old men and old women.

He could see how their features resembled his.

He could see their eyes. Whenever one looks long
and deep into another's eyes, he sees the soul. In looking
deep into the souls of these, his own brothers and sisters,
he could see the anguish

> and the pain
> and the weariness
> and the hopelessness

of a people who had done nothing more to deserve this
cruelty than to just exist.

He saw a happy, energetic, peaceful people whose
only crime was to love and have children and cultivate
their fields and graze their flocks until their home in the
delta had become the envy of all of Egypt.

Moses looked to the edge of the field. In the distance he saw a young man emerge from behind a pile of stacked bricks. He was crawling on hands and knees—writhing in pain as he attempted to dodge the lacerating blows that were being brutally rained down upon his body.

His master grinned the fiendish grin of sadistic cruelty as he continued to beat upon that hideous looking mass of bloody flesh. He was no longer content to punish. His purpose was to kill.

Moses forgot that he was Moses. He forgot that he was the prince of Egypt, the pharaoh-elect, the yet-to-be-appointed king. In a moment of unbridled rage he struck the unsuspecting Egyptian and then wrapped his strong right arm around the overseer's neck.

He flexed the bulging muscles until he heard the myriad little bones crack and break. He felt the man—one of his subjects—go limp on his arm and then sag slowly, lifelessly to the ground.

Moses had just slain an Egyptian—a nobleman—a lesser ruler of the greatest nation on earth. He had slain him in anger—unrestrained, uncontrolled anger—in the defense of a Hebrew. He had killed an Egyptian to save the life of a slave whose life or death was of no concern whatever to the many gods of Egypt.

To bury a body—an Egyptian
body—in the sand was an
unthinkable and unspeakable
blasphemy.

CHAPTER FIVE

(Exodus 2:1-14)

"He . . . hid [his body] in the sand"
(Exodus 2:12).

Hurriedly, Moses dug a hole in the loose, hot sands of the desert. He rolled the lifeless body with its helmet and whip into the ground and covered it quickly. He then smoothed the sand, placed rows of drying bricks over the shallow grave, and walked briskly back to his chariot.

It had been a thousand years since Egyptians had buried their dead in the sand. Sometimes the poor would be forced to use this primitive method and, of course, the Hebrews laid their loved ones to rest in the desert . . . but not since the days of the earliest dynasties had such a practice been observed in Egypt.

Death in that ancient land was considered the beginning of a new life—a new life in another world. That new life, if proper precautions were taken, was designed to last forever.

Because life on earth was relatively short, the Egyptians built their houses of mud. Since the afterlife was eternal, they built their tombs of stone.

Besides a physical body, Egyptians believed everyone had a soul, called a *ba*, and a spiritual counterpart of themselves called a *ka*. When a person died, his *ba* continued to live on the earth, resting within his body at night. His *ka* traveled back and forth between earth and the other world.

Eternal life depended on both the *ba* and the *ka* being able to identify and eventually reside in the proper body. For this reason, an Egyptian corpse was never just buried in sand. It, of necessity, was preserved by the process of mummification. A face mask, bearing an exact replica of the dead, was placed over the mummy's head to assist the *ka* in making the identification.

Elaborate tombs were built to protect the body from decay and from thieves who would steal the gold and precious objects placed within the burial chamber. The tombs ranged in size from a small burial cave hewn out of stone to a man-made mountain, called a pyramid, for a king.

These burial chambers were always sealed tight. Their entry was hidden except for one small hole near the top, just big enough to allow the *ka* to fly through in its search for its body.

Eternal life was so important that a king would begin the construction of his pyramid as soon as he ascended to the throne. Egyptian farmers would spend as much as twenty-five years during their off-seasons, building an adequate tomb for the pharaoh.

The process of mummification took seventy days during which time the corpse was immersed in brine. The internal organs of the deceased were removed from the body and preserved in canopic jars while the body was carefully embalmed and wrapped so that it could last forever.

To deprive an Egyptian of the rite of mummification was to deprive the body of its eternal life. The *ka* would fly endlessly in search of the *ba*. Since it could never be found, it was destined to an eternal death.

To bury a body—an Egyptian body—in the sand was an unthinkable and unspeakable blasphemy.

Moses had committed an unpardonable sin. This sin, when joined together with his doubtful ancestry and the growing jealousy gnawing away at the bones of a threatened pharaoh meant that the prince—whose future had been filled with such glorious promise—was immediately and irrevocably deposed. He was finished . . . through . . . forgotten.

His recorded deeds, written in hieroglyphs in conspicuous and eminent places would be erased forever. His name, once the greatest in the land, would pass into total obscurity.

Future generations would never hear, or speak, or read of the name of Moses, the man who had nearly ruled the greatest empire earth had ever known.

It meant that the prince would now become a fugitive. The pharaoh-elect would become the hunted and the haunted, and the new obsession of Thutmose III would be the death of his once-illustrious successor.

As Moses looked ahead, it seemed that the perpendicular mountains that surrounded the valley floor had been made for no other purpose than to point to the heavens where his God resided.

CHAPTER SIX

(Exodus 3:1, 2)

"And the angel of the Lord appeared to him in a blazing fire . . . ." (Exodus 3:2).

It was morning. Time to move. Time to move the flock across the plain toward the distant wadi to the east that formed the canyon ranging down the sides of Mount Serbal and Mount Sinai.

Each time he moved toward this awesome range of foreboding mountains he was reminded of another life, another time, another place.

The change in the last forty years had been dramatic.

His flight from the pharaoh, disguised as an Egyptian soldier, had been filled with fright each time his presence had been discovered.

Before fleeing the land of his birth, he had learned the incredible truth about his own history, his family, and his Hebrew lineage.

He had been acclaimed the hero of the Hebrews— the first to ever slay an Egyptian.

He had spent priceless moments in secret with his mother and his aging father. He had spoken with his brother Aaron and sister Miriam.

There had been enough time to hear again the stories of Abraham and Isaac and Jacob.

He learned more of the singular God who had promised to deliver these slaves from their bondage.

All of this he had done in the tense, brief time before he was forced to flee from the wrath of the king.

As a fugitive he had exchanged his place as the adopted son of a queen to become the son-in-law of a priest—Jethro, the priest of Midian, a descendant of Abraham who had settled to the east of Mount Sinai.

His endless days and long nights in the solitude of the desert, leading Jethro's flocks, gave Moses time to reflect upon the stories he had heard. Stories of a Creator-God—greater even than Amun—who required no assistance to hold up the heavens and ignite the sun. He needed no help in lifting the stars to their appointed places.

A powerful God, stronger even than Apis, the bull. A God who purportedly had brought worlds into being by just the words of His mouth.

A more glorious God than even Aten Re. A God who not only shone more brightly than the sun, but by His own power made the sun.

A sovereign God who not only controlled the weather, but who invented the extraordinary patterns of the climates and who could cause storms to occur at will like those described by Job, the prince of the land of Uz.

A Creator-God who not only made man and woman, but had established a unique and enduring relationship with them.

A singular God, somewhat like the one that King Akhenaton had described a century earlier to unbelieving Egyptians.

A God who never engaged in scandalous acts of indecency like so many of the gods of his former land.

One God, strong enough and wise enough to control the entire universe, with a heart that loved and with eyes that saw and with ears that heard. A God with lips that could speak and had spoken often in the past, but who had been strangely silent for centuries.

Moses reflected on the promise that God had made to his ancestor, Abraham—a promise made six hundred years earlier that the Hebrew slaves had never forgotten. A promise to someday make these servile people into a great nation with a land of their own, and a King—a king unlike any that Egypt had ever known. One who would rule with wisdom and fairness over the whole earth forever.

That promise seemed preposterous to Moses. Unthinkable. And yet, that same solemn pledge had been repeated to Abraham's son and grandson, and was as fully believed today as it was on the day it was made.

The fact that news from distant Memphis told of increased bondage and heightened persecution under the new king Amenhotep II made the promise even more distant and unbelievable.

The God that Jethro worshiped was this same God. The same God that Job had spoken of years before. The same God the slaves had served, that Aaron and Miriam had trusted. The same God his mother had spoken of so often.

In the desert he had adopted the ways of the people he had once persecuted. He accepted, with some reservation, the faith of those he once ridiculed.

Moses didn't know this God well, but his heart hungered to know more. His mind groped to understand this one God in whom he had come to believe.

As he looked ahead, it seemed that the perpendicular mountains that surrounded the valley floor had been made for no other purpose than to point to the heavens where his new God resided.

Moses thought these massive columns of red granite that rose from the desert floor were designed to hold up the sky which formed the magnificent temple where his new God was to be found.

The approach was always made with apprehension.

Moses had been here many times before. Each time he felt fear as he walked through the gates of nature's immense temple.

His return to the mount was always necessary. Here the waters from winter rains flowed down the sides of the rocks into the canyon. Here was food—life-giving food for the flocks committed to his care.

He ate his breakfast of hard bread, tightened the belt of his loose-fitting robe, and adjusted the headpiece. With his gnarled and bent acacia staff in hand, his goatskin water bag hanging from his belt, he began again to lead the animals to their place of forage.

Without warning, a muffled explosion shook the silence of the morning.

Moses stopped.

He turned.

In the distance he saw the brilliance of flame—red-hot flame—dancing just above the floor of the desert.

It was coming from the very core of a bush—a thorn bush—an acacia tree. A tree native to Sinai, shaped like an immense umbrella and taller than a camel. A tree with delicate leaves and small globular flowers that stands alone in the vastness of the great wilderness.

The flames rose higher. Even in the presence of the blistering sun he could feel the distant heat.

There was no smoke—just flame.

A flame that persisted and continued to burn without withering a leaf or scorching a twig. A different kind of flame that allowed the delicate little flowers to survive even in the presence of the immense heat.

A flame so bright, so commanding, so compelling, that the rest of the world was obscured by its brilliance. Moses was so distracted that he left his flock and moved toward it as if drawn by some irresistible force that completely relieved him of a will of his own.

Moses was about to get acquainted with the one God he really didn't know.

CHAPTER SEVEN

(Exodus 3:3-4)

"God called to him. . . ." (Exodus 3:4).

Moses threw his arm in front of his face. He peered intently into the flames.

His scattered flock drew close.

He saw nothing—nothing but fire—a fire that continued to burn but refused to consume.

Suddenly a VOICE called out,

"MOSES."

The fugitive-shepherd was stricken by the sound. He leaped back and began searching for its source.

No one had ever spoken his name in this place before. Sheep and goats don't talk.

Bedouins mark their territory well when they graze their flocks. Seldom do they pass within shouting distance of each other.

He knew the location of each of the shepherds under his care. None was scheduled to be anywhere near.

He again shielded his eyes and looked.

He looked behind.

He looked up.

He looked down.

He looked back at the tree. He saw no one.

Again the VOICE called his name.

"MOSES."

It was louder. It was more insistent—more compelling. It reverberated back and forth through the gigantic natural columns of the towering mountains.

Without thinking, Moses responded.

"Here I am."

He spoke to the air, to the rocks, to the mountains. He had no idea who was calling his name, but he answered. He blushed as he realized he seemed to be very much alone except for the animals milling around him.

Then he heard,

"DO NOT COME NEAR HERE. . . ."

The words were close, clear, unmistakable, commanding.

Could it be . . . ? he thought.

Could it be possible? . . . Yes, it is—it's coming from the flames—from within that lone tree. It's coming from that tree that continues to burn, but refuses to die.

He stopped. He stood still. In all his years as general of the armies of Egypt he had never heard a command shouted with such clarity.

No pharaoh had ever spoken with such authority.

He was riveted to the spot. His feet refused to move. His body shook with uncontrollable fear. He had been taken captive by a VOICE. He was the prisoner of an unknown captor. He might as well have been in chains. Moses could not have moved if he'd tried.

He didn't know it, but he was about to enter into one of the most dramatic moments of human history.

The God of heaven was making one of His rare appearances on earth—a house call on a lonely fugitive who was sure that whatever gods there were, they had long since forgotten him.

Moses was about to get acquainted with the One God he really didn't know.

It's hard to believe that a man like Moses would have ever had a limited knowledge of God. Like all ancient Egyptians he had been a polytheist. He had worshiped hundreds of gods—not just one.

He had access to very little information.

The Pentateuch was not available to him.

> Genesis
>> Exodus
>>> Leviticus
>>>> Numbers and
>>>>> Deuteronomy had not been written.

(He is the one who wrote them—later.)

There was no national priesthood—

> no moral law
>> no inscribed religious code
>>> no text of Scripture.

The remarkable story of Job had not even been recorded (Moses probably wrote that, too—later.)

The only information Moses had available had been passed by word of mouth from father to son, and mother to child. Three and one-half centuries is a long time to tell a story without its becoming vague or confused.

Moses had heard the creation story.

He knew about Noah and the great flood. He had even detected signs of that deluge around the peaks of Horeb.

He knew about Abraham and his extraordinary journey from the distant land of the River Euphrates.

He knew about Isaac and his miraculous escape from death.

He knew about Jacob and his twelve sons. He had heard how one of his sons, Joseph, had come to be in Egypt.

But all of this was historical knowledge. Anyone who wanted to could obtain the same information. These were intellectual and academic ideas that had stimulated his brain cells, but never gripped his life.

They were mental concepts, but not experiential realities.

Like most of us, he knew about God, but he didn't know God.

It was now time for God to introduce Himself. It was time to tell things to Moses He had told no other man.

It was time to tell Moses that there was one God who really knew him—all about him—and still had plans to use him.

It was time for Moses to learn that one God was all that his world needed.

It was time for an abbreviated, personalized, experiential course in theology for the man who would go down in history, not as Egypt's pharaoh, but as Israel's deliverer.

Moses would become the world's revealer of God in the same way an apostle by the name of Paul would later become the revealer of Christ.

Forty years of solitary confinement in the prison house of obscurity had prepared Moses well. He was now ready to listen to someone else give the commands.

CHAPTER EIGHT

(Exodus 3:4,5)

". . . Do not come near here. . . ."
(Exodus 3:5).

Many things are curious about the flaming acacia tree in the great and terrible wilderness called Sinai.

The fact that it burned at all was strange. (My wife and I once tried vainly to set fire to an acacia tree in the wilderness of Sinai. I thought it would make a remarkable picture. Regardless of how we tried, however, that green tree refused to burn.)

The fact that the tree was not consumed was extraordinary.

The fact that the tree spoke was miraculous.

The most startling fact of all, however, was what the flaming tree said to the silent Moses.

It had called him by name—clearly, distinctly, unmistakably—twice. The tree had even pronounced his name correctly.

The tree then issued two sharp commands.

"DO NOT COME NEAR HERE. . . ."

"REMOVE THE SANDALS FROM YOUR FEET. . . ."

Generals are not used to taking orders. Pharaohs are not accustomed to restricted areas and "No Trespassing" signs. Princes are seldom requested to remove their sandals. Moses, you remember, had once prepared himself to be one of earth's gods; the world's gods removed their shoes for no one.

Moses no longer considered himself to be anything or anyone of significance.

He had been humbled.

Forty years of solitary confinement in the prison house of obscurity had prepared him well. He was now ready to listen to someone else give the commands.

He was broken—willing to listen—ready to learn. God's timing had been perfect. Moses was now ready.

Desert experiences often do that sort of thing to the people who are forced to endure them.

He kept his distance.

He removed his shoes.

He then heard a declarative statement—a statement filled with mystery. A statement that filled him with awe.

The VOICE said,

"FOR THE PLACE ON WHICH YOU ARE STANDING IS HOLY GROUND."

Holy places were everywhere in Egypt. Every temple had its little sanctuary where the common or ordinary people were not permitted. Some had their holy of holies where even Moses had been denied access.

The word *holy* was not new. The experience certainly was. Holy places in Egypt had always been clearly identifiable. They had been carefully built.

They were the residences of the gods.

Moses looked down. He looked around to see what holy ground looked like. He saw the same thing he had been looking at for forty years—light-colored, coarse sand, covered with small pebbles and stones and rocks and boulders. Occasionally a tuft of grass or a lone acacia tree was visible.

He might see a sand-colored lizard slithering across the smooth surface of a piece of limestone, but nothing more.

The ground didn't look holy or uncommon, and yet this mysterious, captivating VOICE had told him that this ground was holy ground.

Moses didn't know it yet, but this was to be God's first description of His Being as He began introducing Himself to man.

The statement was an awesome and frightening term. It spoke of uniqueness. It suggested distance.

Whenever we introduce a stranger to God, we seldom introduce Him as "Holy".

The word *holy* is often threatening and intimidating. It reminds us that we are something we should not be, or are not something we should be.

The word *holy* is most often defined by its secondary meaning, which suggests moral excellence, sinlessness, blamelessness, absolute perfection, and total purity. These words create distance. They instill fear. They disturb. We know that none of us measure up to that inflexible, invariable standard.

The primary meaning of the word is quite different. It does not in any way minimize the perfectness of God. It does state a basic truth that Moses needed desperately to learn.

In both the Hebrew and the Greek, the word *holy* means "to be set apart," "to be separated from," "to be different."

The VOICE was implying to Moses that this ground may have looked like all the other ground he had stood upon; it may have had the same texture, the same feel, but it was not like any other ground he had ever seen—it was different.

It was different because God had declared it to be different. It was different because the one God who was different stood upon it.

God is different.

There are many characteristics of God that make Him different.

His absolute purity—His moral excellence—

distinguishes Him from all other gods. The gods of Egypt were noted for their scandalous behavior. But not this God—He is different.

The God who spoke from the tree is different. He is unseen, invisible. The gods of Egypt were all visible. They were confined to resident temples where they could always be found and always could be viewed. But not this God.

He is different.

God is different from Amun, and Aten Re, and Osiris and Horus. He is different from the Nile god and the war god and the moon god. He's even different from the gods who called themselves pharaohs.

God is different from man. Man is made in the image or spiritual likeness of God—but not in the exact image. If that were the case, then man would be a replica. Man would be God and God would be man. That was true only of Jesus. God is different from man.

God, the Creator, is different from anything and everything in His creation.

He is unique.

He is incomparable.

He is the Great Unlike.

A little child may ask his father . . . "What is God like? Is He like you, Daddy?"

"In some ways, He's like a daddy. He loves like a daddy, and He gives you what you need like a daddy, but He's different.

"Is He like Mommy?"

"In some ways He's like a mommy. He cares for you like a mommy does, but He's different."

"Can I see Him?"

"No."

"Can I touch Him?"

"No."

"Is God a man?"

"No."

"Is God a woman?"

"No . . . the Bible always refers to Him as a man and speaks of Him as 'He,' 'Him,' and 'His,' so that we can understand Him better—but He's different."

"Does He have eyes like we have?"

"Well, God can see, but He couldn't have eyes like we have because God can see everything and everywhere at the same time. God can even see in the dark. He misses nothing. God is different."

"Does God have ears?"

"Yes, God has ears, but they're not like ours. I can only hear you when you're near. God can hear you when you're far away. He can hear everybody at the same time—clearly and distinctly. If you and I were to talk to God at the same time, He would hear us both. God is different."

"Does God have a daddy?"

"No."

"Does God have a mommy?"

"No. God doesn't need a daddy or a mommy. God can take care of all His needs by Himself. He is different."

We began learning this basic truth about God when we were children.

We learned that,

> the Lord's day
>> the Lord's house
>>> the Lord's possessions
>>>> the Lord's people—were different.

Sunday was always different from other days of the week.

Saturday was different. It preceded Sunday. Saturday was haircut day and bath day and shine-your-shoes day.

Sunday was different because it belonged to the God who was different. The Lord's house was different. I could always run in my house, but I could never run in God's house. It was different.

The VOICE was stating to Moses that He was

different. He was unlike any of the gods on the god shelves of Egypt—unlike any of the multiple gods of Moses' previous life—He was different.

God is the Great Unlike.

That's why statues and images and pictures are so unbecoming of God.

That's why anyone who attempts to imitate God is such a disappointment.

That's why illustrations are so impossible. The moment I say, "God is like . . . " I am finished. There is no completion to that sentence. No description is adequate. No definition is satisfying.

God is the Great Unlike.

He is incomparable.

He is unique.

He is different.

Idolatry is any attempt to give visibility to the invisible One.

When Moses later transcribed the commandments, the ones that proclaimed God's uniqueness were always at the top of the list.

The first commandment that Israel disobeyed was the law forbidding them to fashion an image after any creature and then suggest that the image made by man bore any resemblance to God.

The Israelites, thinking Moses had died on Mount Sinai, remembered the Egyptian god, Apis the bull, the most powerful of all of Egypt's gods. They made an image of gold shaped like him. They worshiped him. They believed only the strongest of Egypt's gods could help them.

When Moses finally descended from Sinai's peak, he saw the golden bull-calf. He smashed the tablets of stone. He melted the golden image in the fire, ground it to powder, mixed it with water, and forced the people to drink it.

Moses was making a statement.

God is not a bull-calf.

God is not *like* a bull-calf.

God's people cannot engage in a typical Egyptian orgy around a golden bull-calf, pretending it's God, because God is different.

The VOICE from the tree had made a statement. It implied to Moses that he could wear his shoes anywhere he wished. He could wear them in the presence of Thutmose III or Amenhotep II. He could wear them in the presence of Amun. But he could not wear them in the presence of God, because—

God was different.

But man still wants to see God

> to hear God
>> to touch God
>>> to handle God.

Like the ancient Egyptians, if man can't find God, he'll invent a god of his own or he'll borrow from another in order to attempt to satisfy the curious, insatiable hunger that lies within us all.

Man will create his own Osiris or Isis. He'll exalt his own stork or cat or ape or hawk. He'll deprive himself and his family of life-giving food to worship his cow. He'll turn everything he owns into his own multiple gods, like the Hindus who worship 330 million such beings. Hindus average no less than eight gods to every family.

Man must not only see his gods, but he must build temples to house his gods. In Thailand alone, Buddhists have built twenty thousand such places. There are more temples in Thailand than there are Christians.

If man cannot find something lofty or great to worship, he will build his temple of Actium in Greece and then sacrifice his oxen to the god of flies.

Man must have a god.

He must be able to see his god.

But God is different. He is invisible, unapproachable and incomparable. How is it possible for the God who is different to maintain His uniqueness and yet satisfy the instinctive longing of humanity's curious heart?

Jesus is the answer.

God wrapped Himself in human flesh and placed Himself on display. There is a painting in a palace in Rome by Reni. It is painted into the ceiling of the dome which rises to a height of more than 100 feet. To stand at floor level and look upward is extremely difficult. The position is uncomfortable, and the painting seems to be surrounded by a fog which obscures and diminishes its brilliance.

To correct the problem and to bring the painting within the range of human vision, a large, highly polished mirror was installed directly beneath the giant dome. By looking down into the mirror, every detail of the magnificent painting can be studied with satisfaction and with ease.

Jesus is the mirror of God—the precise image of His Person—the exact replica of His Being. Jesus details God with such accuracy that it was possible for Him to say, ". . . He who has seen Me has seen the Father" (John 14:9).

John goes even further to exclaim man's complete satisfaction by stating that He has not only seen God through Christ, but He has also heard Him and handled Him. (1 John 1:1-2)

God is different.

Distant—but not aloof.

He bridged the distance completely in Christ and made Himself accessible to us all. He is beyond the reach of no one.

God is different. He is confined to no locality but is visible and available to all.

**People like to make gods, but
God likes to make people.**

CHAPTER NINE

(Exodus 3:6)

"... Moses ... was afraid to look at God" (Exodus 3:6).

Someone once asked me, "When did Moses become a Christian?"

We all know that the term *Christian* is one reserved for the followers of Christ. Since Moses lived on earth long before Jesus did, the term is hardly appropriate to Moses—and yet I knew what the questioner was asking.

When did Moses finally acknowledge his sin—his unworthiness—his great need? When did he fully surrender his life to God?

When did the God of Abraham become the God of Moses?

Right here—in Exodus, chapter 3, verse 6—just a few moments after Moses was made aware of God's uniqueness.

The VOICE finally introduced itself—not by name but by reputation. God dropped some names that were familiar to Moses. Names used by the Hebrews. Names that God used as He began displaying His credentials to the fugitive from Egypt.

Again, He declared His uniqueness.

Moses was accustomed to relating the gods of Egypt to *things*. There was

> the god of the moon
> the god of the sun
> the god of the Nile
> the god of the beetle
> the god of war
> the god of life, and
> the god of death.

The gods of Egypt were identified with visible objects or common experiences that were all a part of that ancient culture.

When the VOICE finally introduced Himself, He identified Himself not with things, but with *people*.

He said,

> I AM THE GOD OF YOUR FATHERS, THE GOD OF ABRAHAM, THE GOD OF ISAAC, AND THE GOD OF JACOB.

The VOICE identified itself. This was God speaking. And, this God who was speaking was a personal God, a God of relationships, a people-God.

He identified Himself as the One Moses' father had talked about. The One his grandfather had talked about. All his ancestors as far back as six hundred years had claimed a special relationship with this God.

What kind of people were these people who claimed a relationship with this different kind of God?

Were they a different kind of people?

Were they unique, incomparable?

Were they a special breed—a distinct race?

A perfect God doesn't choose imperfect people, does He? Does a God who is different allow Himself to relate to a people who are common?

Does God choose a people because they are different, or does He choose a people and then make them different?

Abraham wasn't particularly different from his generation. He lived in the very cradle of civilization—in

Ur of the Chaldees. He lived along the Euphrates River in a pagan civilization, much like Moses had lived along the Nile in a land of many gods.

Abraham was an idolater like his father—and like Moses. He knew little or nothing about the God of the Flaming Tree.

Isaac was not unique. He is famous for nothing more than for being the son of Abraham. He is a nonentity in Scripture—more passive than active.

He is pictured in his declining years as being self-indulgent and susceptible to the crudest forms of deception.

Jacob was the deceptive one. He deceived his father, his brother, his sister-in-law, and anyone else who had something he wanted. He was always stealing something that didn't belong to him. He even stole his brother's inheritance and his brother's blessing.

None of these three with whom God identified Himself would appear at first—or even later—to be good candidates for heaven's Hall of Fame.

Abraham didn't meet the qualifications for being the human father of a superhuman race. He had none of the physical qualifications for creating a spiritual people.

Neither Isaac nor Jacob was qualified for the promises that ultimately became theirs.

All of these had great defects of character—great blots on their conduct. At times they appeared as moral cripples, and yet God established a relationship with them—a unique and permanent relationship. One that had lasted six hundred years and was destined to last forever.

God didn't choose these men because they were different. He chose them and then made them different. They weren't chosen because they were great. They were chosen and then made great.

God is different, isn't He?

People like to make gods. People make them out of wood and stone. They make them out of gold and silver. They make them out of animals and birds and fish.

People make gods out of their memories, and they make gods out of their dreams. People like to make gods. Gods they can see and feel. Gods they can talk to but who can't talk back. Making gods is an obsession with people —an obsession from which all of us need to be delivered.

God likes to make people—great people out of common people . . . strong people out of weak people . . . famous people out of unknown people . . . good people out of bad people.

God likes to make people. That's an obsession with God. One from which He will never change.

Abraham, Isaac, and Jacob are examples of people whom God made. He made them from nothing into something. God gave them privileged places in history and then proudly referred to them whenever He wanted to make Himself known.

God makes people into not only what He wants them to be, but also into what they have always wanted to become.

And now He was about to make Moses—about to make him into someone far above the heads of all the pharaohs, and far beyond even Moses' wildest dreams.

What kind of people does God relate Himself to?

Imperfect people. There are no other kind. Imperfect people like you and like me. People whom God loves in spite of imperfections and whom God helps to become free of imperfections.

What kind of people does God relate Himself to?

Living people!

Like all of Egypt's rulers, Moses wanted to live forever. A proper burial and a foolproof tomb were part of the process, he thought.

This new God—this God of the Flaming Tree—this God of Abraham, Isaac and Jacob—was now making a staggering claim. He was claiming to be the God of the people who live forever.

When He stated,

"I AM THE GOD OF   ," He was talking about

being the present God of people out of the past. Abraham was dead. Isaac was dead. Jacob was dead. They had been dead for centuries—or had they?

According to this remarkable statement, these men, like their God, were very much alive.

"I AM" is present tense. It refers to the eternal present. The present that never slips into the past.

God is the God of the living—not of the dead.

Abraham was not dead.

Isaac was not dead.

Jacob was not dead.

They had all been buried, but they were not dead. They were all three as much alive as was this God who was speaking. There was no need for the embalmers to preserve anything. No opening was needed in the peak of a burial chamber for a *ka* to find its way back.

The living God had made provision to be the God of the living. He knew how to keep His people alive forever—and He does!

And it was not just a *ka* or a *ba* that was to be kept alive. It was the whole being. A transformed body, a living soul, and an eternal spirit would experience neverending life in a real, definable, describable place. It was not some nether world or never-never land, as the Egyptians believed. It was not reincarnation in another form in another life. It was to be a resurrection in a perfect form forever.

Imperfect people!

Living people!

Bad people who can be changed, and dead people who can continue to live.

That's the amazing declaration God made in a simple twenty-one-word introduction of Himself.

God is different, isn't He?

How did Moses react to this revelation?

Moses was stunned.

Standing in the presence of the Great Unlike, the incomparable, the One and Only among all the gods, the

One who is perfect in purity and in righteousness, eternal, and who makes His followers to live forever, was too much for the ex-prince.

Moses was immediately aware that his whole being—

> his past
>> his present
>>> his future
>>>> his thoughts
>>>>> his plans
>>>>>> his works
>>>>>>> his deeds

were exposed to the limitless scrutiny of a holy God.

The fugitive running from his pharaoh was suddenly caught in the brilliant glare of God's all-encompassing searchlight. He was morally blinded by the brightness that enveloped him.

"Moses hid his face for he was afraid to look at God."

This was the beginning of Moses' ministry.

Both his life and his ministry began at the same moment. They began with a clear, concise recognition of need—plus a clear, concise revelation of God.

Moses' life-changing experience came in the barrenness of the remote desert of Midian, right at the base of the forbidding cliffs of Sinai.

A similar thing happened to Isaiah. His new life began in Jerusalem at four o'clock in the afternoon, near the gate of the Temple. Isaiah stood within the area where sacrifices were made. It was there, in mid-life, that his epochal moment arrived.

He saw God, elevated and exalted. He saw Him seated upon His throne surrounded by angelic beings.

He heard the magnificent voices of heavenly beings singing in one great antiphonal choir about God's holiness and His indescribable glory.

The decibel level was so high that the very foundations of the thresholds vibrated in response to the thunderous sounds, and the Temple itself filled with smoke.

He saw himself as ruined and unclean and unworthy, and he repented of his sin and was forgiven. (See Isaiah 6:1-7.)

Job's life began when he was seventy—in a garbage dump—after months of agonizing pain and rejection.

God appeared in the midst of a whirlwind in the presence of flashing lightning and resounding thunder. The heavens had let loose, and the earth was deluged. Darkness had engulfed His whole creation when suddenly, from the midst of heaven's awesome spectacle, God spoke. As He spoke, each word of the seventy questions He addressed to Job drove the complainer lower and lower into the dust of Uz until finally in deep humiliation he threw ashes over his whole body and cried out, "I retract, I repent." (cf. Job 40, 41, 42)

For the apostle Paul, life began on a mountainous road north of Jerusalem, north of Galilee—the road to the ancient city of Damascus.

In his self-righteous delusion, Saul of Tarsus was determined that it was his responsibility to rid the world of Christians—to liquidate the followers of The Way—to exterminate humanity's infectious pests. This, he was convinced, was his reason for being—his service to God.

On the outskirts of Damascus, en route to imprison any that he found, he was suddenly blinded by a great light. He fell to the ground. The same God who had spoken from the flaming acacia tree at the base of Sinai spoke to Saul, and clearly identified Himself. So it was that the avowed enemy of Christians became one himself.

The God whom he thought he knew and whom he thought he worshiped broke through that day and blinded this zealot. In a moment . . . he saw the God he really didn't know, and became His captive.

These men all worshiped the same God, but didn't really know Him. Their lives were changed when they were exposed to their need and God was revealed to their being.

It was then that Moses was changed—when there was nothing left to do but to submit and surrender.

He, like King Occhoris of Ethiopia, was now the captive of One greater and stronger than himself. His struggles to *become* now ceased, and he finally gave in to God.

The God of Abraham, Isaac, and Jacob had finally become the God of Moses.

God knows. He knows both the problem and its solution. That knowledge, coupled with His power, makes Him infinitely different from any and all other gods.

CHAPTER TEN

(Exodus 3:7-9)

"... I am aware of their sufferings" (Exodus 3:7).

Moses recovered slowly.

God waited.

When Moses was ready to hear, God continued to speak.

I HAVE SURELY SEEN THE AFFLICTION OF MY PEOPLE WHO ARE IN EGYPT, AND HAVE GIVEN HEED TO THEIR CRY BECAUSE OF THEIR TASKMASTERS, FOR I AM AWARE OF THEIR SUFFERINGS (Exodus 3:7).

The Exodus began in the heart and mind of God. Deliverance always begins with God. The timing and even the process are always God's.

Moses knew the plight of the two million Hebrew hostages. He knew it firsthand; he knew it well.

He had been part of the cause. He had tried to be part of the solution, but had failed miserably.

Moses knew how Amenhotep II had tightened his grip on the beleaguered nation. He had received only brief and sporadic reports, but he knew.

What Moses didn't know was that God knew. He had no idea that the God of Abraham, Isaac, and Jacob had been watching all the time.

God said,

> I HAVE SURELY SEEN THE AFFLICTION OF MY PEOPLE WHO ARE IN EGYPT. . . .

Only brief, inadequate reports had drifted across the desert. But God said,

> I HAVE SEEN . . .

The phrase suggests continuance. It could read, "Seeing I have seen." It means that God has been watching without interruption. His was not just a casual glance, not just an abbreviated report from a subordinate. It was a personal, round-the-clock inspection. God had continually surveyed every inch of the six thousand square miles that comprise the Delta region where the Hebrews lived. He had watched them at work in the treasure cities of Pithom and Rameses. He had watched the very field above Memphis where Moses had witnessed the brutal beatings of many. He saw them as servants in the homes of the nobles as far south as Thebes. He saw them all—everywhere, continuously.

He heard their sighs—that's silent grief.

He heard their cries—that's noisy grief.

He heard their groans—that's the rasping, cacophonous sound that rolls off the lips. It is sound without meaning, sound without sense. It is the sound of persistent, unending pain—pain that has neither source nor relief. It is sound that constantly speaks of a hurt way down inside—so deep that it's beyond the reach of healing and even beyond the scope of understanding.

God heard their cries for help—that's the persistent and agonizing pleading for someone, somewhere, to come to the rescue.

God heard it all.

He also saw the heartless, barbarous acts of babies being torn from their mothers' arms, ruthlessly slain, and then thrown into the muddy waters of the Nile.

He saw some of the babies, still alive, being thrown to the waiting, hungry jaws of the crocodiles.

Nothing escapes the attention of God—nothing! God saw every Hebrew man, every Hebrew woman, every Hebrew child—clearly and distinctly, collectively and separately. He saw every cruel act—every unkind deed.

He not only saw the hand that delivered it, but the heart that prompted it.

The God of perfect, undistorted vision, who never even takes time to blink His penetrating eyes, saw it all.

In Exodus 2:25 it also says that God not only saw and knew, but it adds the perplexing words: "God took notice of them."

These words are not suggesting that God kept a record or took notes. God's recall is perfect—no notes are necessary. It means that God knew what was happening. He knew all that was happening. He knew how long it had been going on and just how much longer it would last. He knew, not only intellectually, but experientially.

He was not just aware—not just passively observing—He was entering right into their suffering. He was feeling their pain. He was hurting—not only for them, but with them.

Recently I went through the trauma of having a cancer removed from my left arm just above the elbow. What had appeared to be an innocent-looking skin lesion was diagnosed as a melanoma.

The word dropped like concrete into my brain, set up quickly, and hardened as a permanent, grim, and ominous reminder of my mortality.

A good friend had died of melanoma. My father had died of cancer. My two brothers had both had major cancer surgery—and now I had a melanoma.

I read the statistics from the American Cancer Society. Seventeen thousand Americans will contract melanoma this year—five thousand will die.

The survival percentages were carefully analyzed by my doctor, but passed right over my head. Eighty percent chance of survival. Good odds, but they were completely dismissed. I only heard him describe the 20 percent chance of fatality.

It was weeks before we were sure of the success of the surgery. Weeks of anxiety. Weeks of uncertainty.

As one doctor was dressing my arm, carrying out his role with remarkable knowledge, skill, and tenderness, I asked him, "Doctor, have you ever had cancer?"

He looked at me for a long time before dropping his eyes. He then said, "No, I've never had cancer. My mother has cancer, but I've never had cancer."

His masterful skill was immediately limited. Limited to the physical process of healing for which he was so well trained and thoroughly equipped. He was forced to admit his inability to completely understand—an inability God has never known.

I asked my surgeon the same question the next day. John Zook lifted his eyes from his work and answered, "Yes . . . I've had cancer." He then put down his instruments and showed me the scars between his right thumb and forefinger—on his surgeon's hand, placing his life—his skill—his whole future in jeopardy.

His eyes moistened as he put his arm around me and said again, "Yes, Don, I've had cancer."

He knew. He understood. Experience made it possible to enter into my anxiety-ridden soul and to "feel" with me.

God sees, God hears, God knows, God understands. God even feels what we're feeling.

God was telling Moses that He had researched every incident, every scene.

He had recalled every sound, every sigh, every word.

He had gathered every tear into His special little tear bottle.

He had punched it all into His infinite memory bank.

God is different, isn't He?

Unlike the ancient Egyptian gods who had eyes, but saw not —ears, but heard not—gods who had mouths, but spoke not. Unlike the gods who had never felt anything, God had experienced it all.

God is not only different, morally excellent, and interested primarily in people, but God knows.

In theology class we called that *omniscience*.

> God knows all—
>> past
>>> present, and
>>>> future.

He knew exactly what was taking place in Egypt in the life of every person during every single moment of every single day.

He knew what was happening in Midian.

He knew right where to find Moses.

He knew what it would take to catch his attention.

He knew his name—and how to pronounce it.

He knew just the right moment when Moses would be ready to listen.

God *knows*.

He knows His creation.

He knows just how many stars there are, and has a name for each.

He knows His creatures. Not one sparrow falls without His knowledge.

He sees all the sons of men.

He knows our every thought.

He knows our needs and can distinguish them from our wants.

He has already counted the hairs on our head.

God knows.

God's knowledge is immediate. It's not inductive or deductive. It's not acquired by observation.

God sees, yet He knows without seeing.

Ancient Egyptians represented one of their gods as being just an eye—not having an eye, but being an eye.

Our dollar bills display an eye atop a pyramid. It's open and it sees.

God even knows where that dollar bill goes.

God knows

> before it happens—
> while it's happening—
> after it's finished.

God knows

> what happened—
> what didn't happen—
> what could have happened and
> what should have happened.

God knows.

No one says it better than A. W. Tozer: "God possesses perfect knowledge and has no need to learn. God has never learned and cannot learn, for there is nothing God does not know."[1]

God knows all

> perfectly,
> instantly,
> completely.

He knows

> our sin,
> our suffering,
> our affliction, and
> our adversity.

We are always within the observation of God.

To those who have something to hide, that's frightening.

To those who need understanding, that's a source of great comfort.

God knows and God understands, but again, He is different.

Unlike many who have knowledge, and even unlike many who understand, God is capable of doing something about it.

The VOICE continued,

> SO I HAVE COME DOWN TO DELIVER THEM FROM THE POWER OF THE EGYPTIANS, AND TO BRING THEM UP FROM THAT LAND TO A GOOD AND SPA-

CIOUS LAND, TO A LAND FLOWING WITH MILK
AND HONEY, TO THE PLACE OF THE CANAANITE
AND THE HITTITE AND THE AMORITE AND THE
PERIZZITE AND THE HIVITE AND THE JEBUSITE
(Exodus 3:8).

God not only knew conditions in Egypt and Midian,
but He also knew conditions in the land of promise—and
more. He knew just how the Hebrews were going to get
there, and when.

God knows. His knowledge of both the problem and
the solution, coupled with His power to deliver, make Him
infinitely different from any other and all other gods.

Annie Johnson Flint wrote,

> I know not, but God knows;
> Oh, blessed rest from fear!
> All my unfolding days
> To Him are plain and clear.
> Each anxious, puzzled "why?"
> From doubt or dread that grows,
> Finds answers in this thought:
> I know not, but He knows.

We've all been noticing lately the increasing emphasis
being placed on America's missing children. I see their
beautiful faces everywhere—on television, in newspap-
ers, on posters, and even on milk cartons.

The heartache one feels from the sadness of this
ugly national disaster is only tempered by the realization
that to God, they are not missing—not lost. He knows—
He knows. He knows where they are and how they are.
That is not as satisfying to heartbroken parents as their
return. But it does provide some measure of comfort.

God knows.

Chapter 10, Notes

1. A.W. Tozer, *The Knowledge of the Holy* (New York: Harper & Bros.,
1961), p. 61.

The God who is different from all of us, was about to join Himself to one of us.

CHAPTER ELEVEN

(Exodus 3:10)

". . . I will send you. . . ." (Exodus 3:10).

If there is anything we need during any of life's baffling or bewildering experiences, it is not an explanation, but just a fresh, new look at God.

That's what Moses was getting.

The longer he looked, the more he saw.

The longer he listened to that loud, clear, resonant VOICE coming from the miracle tree in the distance, the more he realized that this God was truly different.

The surprises had just begun. The biggest and most overwhelming was yet to come.

The VOICE spoke again,

THEREFORE, COME NOW, AND I WILL SEND YOU TO PHARAOH, SO THAT YOU MAY BRING MY PEOPLE, THE SONS OF ISRAEL, OUT OF EGYPT (Exodus 3:10).

God was about to establish a unique relationship with man. It was an I-You relationship. This different God was about to link Himself up with the barefoot shepherd standing in the blistering sand at the base of Mount Sinai.

The God who is different from all of us was about to join Himself to one of us.

God, who is morally excellent, pure, blameless, without sin and without guilt, was about to link Himself with a man who was a polytheist—who believed in many gods—a man who was a runaway fugitive from Egypt—a murderer who had killed a civil servant in cold blood and buried his body in the sand.

Not only had Moses killed an Egyptian, he was also party to the deaths of thousands of Hebrews prior to that.

It's interesting to me to note that the two most significant men in both the Old and New Testaments—

> Moses—the revealer of God, and
> Paul—the revealer of Christ

were murderers.

Both Moses and Paul had killed those who were very special to God.

Moses killed Hebrews—the Old Covenant children of God.

Paul killed Christians—the New Covenant children of God.

Both were murderers. I mentioned this fact to a group of singles. Someone responded with an unsigned note that read,

> It's sure a good thing Moses was only a murderer and not divorced or he never would have been able to serve the Lord.

If Josephus is correct, Moses had even been married—to an Egyptian girl whom he must have left behind when he fled Egypt. We don't know that. The Scriptures are silent.

We do know Moses was a murderer.

The same man who spoke the words,

> "Thou shalt not kill . . ."

was a killer.

How can a God who is different, who commands us not to kill, use a killer to be one of earth's greatest spiritual leaders?

How can a holy God use an unholy people to do holy work?

Before answering that, we should probably remind ourselves that God has no other kind of people available.

The answer is found in one word—five letters—GRACE. In sending Moses the murderer to represent Him, God is confronting us with the mystery of mysteries, called grace—God's grace.

The word is as inexhaustible as it is indefinable. I have all sorts of definitions available, but I must confess I still don't really know what it means.

We can call grace—

> "God's unmerited favor,"
> "God's undeserved kindness,"
> "God operating toward man in love," or,
> "God's riches at Christ's expense."

All good definitions—but all inadequate.

Dr. A. W. Tozer says,

> Grace is the good pleasure of God that inclines Him to bestow benefits upon the undeserving—
> to pity the wretched,
> to spare the guilty,
> to welcome the outcast.

I like that. He goes on to say,

> Grace originates in the heart of God but flows out to men through Jesus Christ.[1]

Dr. J. I. Packer says,

> Grace is a personal activity of God—God operating manwards—a spontaneous, self-determined kindness which is unknown to Greek and Roman ethics and theology (it was unknown in Egypt, too), but today is the staple diet in our Sunday Schools and in our churches. We sing it routinely

in our hymns. We read it repeatedly in Scripture—but very few of us actually believe in grace."[2]

Moses didn't believe in grace. Moses knew nothing about grace. His first reaction to God's preposterous call was sheer unbelief.

Notice what he said,

Who am I, that I should go to Pharaoh, and that I should bring the sons of Israel out of Egypt? (Exodus 3:11).

"Who me? Surely God can't mean me." These incredulous thoughts raced through his mind. Moses was convinced that the God who knew everything about everyone should know enough about Moses to realize that he was

ineligible,
    unworthy, and
        disqualified.

Moses was an outcast, a murderer, and a fugitive. Moses was guilty. His was not imagined guilt. His was real guilt. He was a killer. When God made it known that His plan was to use Moses, the fugitive's reaction was that this was the most preposterous idea he had ever heard.

Like most of us, Moses had lived his entire life on a performance level—"If I do right, live right, think right, the gods will be pleased with me. If I do not, the gods will be displeased with me."

Moses remembered Osiris.

Osiris was the Egyptian god who sat in the hall of judgment with forty-two assessors. Their job was to weigh the deeds of the dead. Osiris was the supreme judge.

Anubis, the god with the body of a man and the head of a jackal, held a pair of scales in his hand.

The dead man listed all the things he had not done in life —the crimes he had not committed. The man's heart was on one balance, the feather of truth was on the other. If the heart, heavy with guilt, outweighed the feather, the man was condemned. His heart was immediately eaten by Amit, a god with the head of a crocodile. The guilty man could not live in the after-life. He was destroyed forever.

Moses, from his youth, believed what he'd been taught. If one's good deeds outweigh the bad, he would live forever. If not, his punishment would be swift and eternal.

It's amazing how many of us have been indoctrinated with the pagan beliefs of ancient Egypt. Many still think in terms of scales and balances. If our God judged in this way, we would all be lost forever. No deeds are good enough to outweigh the ultimate insult mankind paid to God when Adam and Eve chose to worship a lesser god called Satan.

The only way this gross sin could be forgiven was for God to pay the penalty Himself in the Person of His Son, Jesus Christ, and then *give* eternal life to those who would receive Jesus as God's provision for man's sin.

Grace is God's obsession to give—God's constraining desire to reach out to the untouchable and provide for his need.

Moses was about to learn that performance was not enough.

He was about to learn that God had a different plan—a plan that was as dependent upon God's grace before Jesus died as it was after His death.

Moses was about to learn that God's plan would even allow a murderer who had acknowledged his sin and who had accepted forgiveness to be linked together with the Holy One to represent Him to an unholy world.

Most of us really don't believe in grace.

For example,

> If I still believe
>   that if my good deeds outweigh my bad deeds,
>   I'll be saved—

I don't believe in grace (Ephesians 2:8,9).
If I still believe
    that belonging to a church—any church—will
      save me—
I don't believe in grace (John 3:7).
If I still believe
    that I'm saved by confirmation, church mem-
      bership,
      the sacraments or the ordinances—
I don't believe in grace (Titus 3:5).
If I still believe
    that I'm saved by grace through faith but that
      my
      salvation is secured by my obedience
      to the law—
I don't believe in grace (Galatians 3:3).
If I still believe
    that I'm saved by grace and then can lose that
      salvation by anything that I do or do
      not do—
I don't believe in grace (John 10:28, 29).

Grace teaches us that God gives freely and fully in response to our repentance and faith.

Grace teaches us that God gives.

God gives, not according to my performance,

    my good works,
      my heritage,
        my color, or
          my culture.

God gives because He wants to give.

God gives because He chooses to give.

God is free to give because, even during Moses' lifetime, Jesus was the Lamb of God slain before the foundation of the world.

Moses was as dependent upon Christ's death for forgiveness—though that sacrifice had not yet been offered—as are we today, two thousand years after the sacrifice was offered on Calvary.

It's so easy to drift into performance-level thinking. It's possible to teach our children the pagan doctrines of ancient Egypt without even realizing it.

To suggest to our children that

"God will not love you if . . ."

or

"You won't be a Christian if . . ."

or even

"Christians don't do things like that . . ."

is to teach them untruth—an untruth that obscures the message of God's grace.

Moses was disqualified, ineligible. He had failed. He was convicted for life. The sentence had been imposed. There was no reprieve, no pardon—but that was before he heard of God's grace.

The truth is, we've all been disqualified. If God did not approach us through grace—if God did not give us salvation as a free gift—none of us could ever serve Him.

Chuck Swindoll tells the story of Jack Holcomb, singer-evangelist who had just finished a series of meetings in southern Colorado. The meetings had been such a success they had been moved from a church to a large arena.

His next meeting was in Waco, Texas.

He left—late on Sunday night—tired, irritable, in a hurry—speeding.

Holcomb looked in his rearview mirror and saw an ominous flashing red light. He heard the wail of the police siren.

He pulled over. The officer walked up to the side of the car and said, "May I . . ."

That was all he was able to say before the evangelist interrupted him with, "Look, officer, no lectures—I know I was speeding. Just give me the ticket and get it over with."

The officer stepped back and ordered Holcomb out of the car. "Place your hands on top of the car; please spread your legs." The officer went through the humiliating process of searching him.

He then turned Jack Holcomb around, told him to put his arms down and said, "You know, I used to be just like you, but a week and a half ago I made the greatest decision of my life. I attended a series of meetings in Colorado Springs and I trusted Jesus Christ as my God and Savior. I really wondered as I watched your driving, and now as I see your anger—is there some way I can be of help to you?"

Jack Holcomb looked at the officer and then dissolved in tears. "I am the one who led you to Christ," he said.

> Disqualified?
> > Unfit?
> > > Finished?
> > > > Ineligible?

Grace teaches us to live godly lives and to be responsible people, but grace also teaches that God

> saves us in spite of our sin—
> uses us in spite of our mistakes—
> indwells us in spite of our humanness—
> leads us in spite of our rebellion—and
> loves us in spite of our rejection.

Jesus Christ is the extension of God that spans the distance between God and man, and allows God's power and God's life to flow into believing humanity.

Grace says that God gives. God gave His Son, Jesus, in order that He might give His love and His forgiveness to all who receive His Son.

Moses was about to learn that God was giving him something he never deserved and never could have earned. Another chance.

A chance to link up with God regardless of his past, a chance to accept God's forgiveness and then display God's power to a watching world.

Moses was about to learn the meaning of grace.

Chapter 11, Notes

1. A.W. Tozer, *Knowledge of the Holy* (New York: Harper & Bros., 1961), p. 100.
2. J.I. Packer, *Knowing God* (Downers Grove, Ill.: InterVarsity Press, 1973), p. 116.

God never calls any of us to anything by ourselves. God always provides companionship. No one serves God in isolation.

CHAPTER TWELVE

(Exodus 3:11, 12)

". . . I will be with you. . . ." (Exodus 3:12).

God was still speaking.

The bush was still burning.

Moses was still a captive caught completely in the miracle of it all. God was doing with Moses the same thing He did with the apostle Paul fifteen hundred years later—in the same Arabian desert. He was giving him a thorough course in biblical theology. He was teaching Moses about Himself.

To God's five-letter word, *grace*, Moses responded not only with guilt, but also with fear.

Moses had been one of the world's revered leaders— a military genius who launched successful campaigns in every direction.

He was noted for his skill, his daring, his raw courage. He would lead armies from the deck of his speeding chariot, sword flashing, lances flying, and never once flinch in the face of the enemy.

He had stood in the presence of the world's kings and had commanded their respect.

He had knelt before Egypt's gods and made demands of them that no other human would dare suggest.

But now . . . he had failed and he had fled.

This single failure had erased all memory of his long string of successes. His one failure had stripped him of his confidence.

Failure has a habit of doing that, doesn't it?

Moses was afraid. For forty years he had dwelt on one memory.

He had recalled it,

    relived it,
      savored it.

He chewed on it over and over again. He had thought of it so often that it was the only remaining memory he had of Egypt.

He had failed.

I experienced similar feelings of fear when Hinson Church called me to be their pastor many years ago.

The church had a great history, a ministry with worldwide influence, and had boasted a long list of prestigious and powerful pastors.

Then they called me.

I came fresh out of what I considered a failure experience. I had just been released from the psychiatric ward of a veterans hospital, having been severely depressed for nearly four years.

I had resigned my pastorate because of depression.

I had assumed that my public ministry was finished, or at least significantly limited.

I felt woefully inadequate, and the embarrassment of failure hung over me like a dark cloud.

I was certain that my failure would be repeated—but thankfully it was not.

Most of us have failed, and most of us have memory banks that find it so much easier to store up the negative memories of failure.

I can get a hundred compliments only to have them all erased by one criticism.

I can experience a hundred victories, all of which can be swept away by one defeat.

I can hear a hundred people say, "I love you," and have them all buried beneath one intimidating frown or scowl.

I can preach a hundred times with poise and power and then lose the joy of the pulpit with just one miserable performance.

Moses had failed. He was immobilized by fear. When he answered God with the words,

> Who am I that I should go to Pharaoh, and that I should bring the Sons of Israel out of Egypt?

he was also saying,

I can't do it!
The job's too much for me.
I failed once, I'll fail again.

God loves to use failures.

He delights in doing the unexpected. The apostle Paul reminds us that God uses weak people and foolish people in preference to the strong and the wise.

God had chosen the world's least likely candidate to launch a one-man invasion upon Egypt and bring about the release of a captive nation.

What did God offer Moses in return for his reluctance?

Rebuke? Shame? Insistence?

No, none of these.

To the guilt-ridden Moses, God had offered His grace.

To the fearful Moses, God offered His companionship.

The VOICE again spoke. It seemed that every time God spoke the fire burned brighter . . . the flame became more intense . . . the heat more stifling. The flames leaped and danced with renewed brilliance in response to each word that God spoke.

CERTAINLY I WILL BE WITH YOU. . . . (Exodus 3:12).

The same VOICE that established a relationship promised companionship.

These were strange and foreign words to Moses. The words, "I will be with you," suggested that God was a portable God—a mobile Being.

He could move about with ease, and at will.

He was not stationary like the gods of ancient Egypt. The resident gods of his former life never moved. Their location was always predictable—it never changed.

Moses was learning a new truth—an exciting truth—from his fresh, new look at God.

> God is not confined to one location.
> God is not limited to one place.
> God is not bound to one spot.
> God is omnipresent.

> God in the totality of His essence, without diffusion or expansion, multiplication or division, penetrates and fills the universe in all of its parts.[1]

Omnipresence means that God is everywhere present and nowhere absent.

> He is here—
>   He is there—
>   He is everywhere.

> There is no place where God is not. God is everywhere here. He is close to everything, and next to everyone.[2]

> He is here—
>   He is there—
>   He is everywhere.

He is closer to us than our thoughts—closer to us than ourselves.

A local god is no real god. If God is not everywhere, He is not true God anywhere.

This was God's message to a fearful failure.

God said the same thing to Moses, "I will be with you . . ." that Jesus said to the church as He launched His great redemptive program—"I am with you always. . . ." (Matthew 28:20).

God never calls anyone to do anything without providing companionship. No one serves God in isolation.

He always has company. God is always present.

> He is here—
>> He is there—
>>> He is everywhere.

When my children, John and Kathy, were small, there were times when the darkness or the unknown was too forbidding—too frightening to endure alone. Often they would say, "Daddy— Mommy—I'm scared, will you go with me?" All they required was a second person. Fears immediately melted away.

God had just promised to be that "second person" to Moses. He had said,

CERTAINLY I WILL BE WITH YOU.

That's a timeless promise, you know. It's not limited in time to an episode 3,400 years back in history or confined to a man called Moses.

That promise is as up-to-date as today, and embraces all.

David, the psalmist, asked the question,

> Where can I go from Thy Spirit?
> Or where can I flee from Thy presence?

With firm conviction and without hesitation, he answered,

> If I ascend to heaven, Thou art there;
> If I make my bed in Sheol, behold, Thou art there.
> If I take the wings of the dawn,
> If I dwell in the remotest part of the sea,
> Even there Thy hand will lead me,
> And Thy right hand will lay hold of me
>> (Psalm 139:7-10).

> God is here—
>> God is there—
>>> God is everywhere.

Chapter 12, Notes

1. P.H. Strong, *Systematic Theology* (Philadelphia: Judson Press, 1907), p. 279.
2. A.W. Tozer, *The Knowledge of the Holy* (New York: Harper & Bros., 1961), p. 79.

God lives in the timeless present—the everlasting now. With God there is no past—there is no future.

CHAPTER THIRTEEN

(Exodus 3:13)

"... I am who I am ..." (Exodus 3:14).

Who are You?
What is Your name?
All gods have a name. I can't just tell Pharaoh or even the sons of Israel that a flaming tree talked to me—that a burning bush sent me back to Egypt to rescue the Hebrews.

These were the thoughts racing through Moses' mind as he asked,

> Behold, I am going to the sons of Israel, and I shall say to them, "The God of your fathers has sent me to you." Now they may say to me, "What is His name?" What shall I say to them? (Exodus 3:13).

A breathless moment had arrived. God was being asked a question He could not dodge—a question no one had ever asked before.

God, the uniquely different, morally excellent people-God, who is all-knowing, gracious, and everywhere present, was about to tell man His name.

He had never before revealed His personal name. God had been called by many titles and by compound names with significant meanings. But prior to that moment, He had never revealed His personal name.

The name appears here for the first time in Scripture. It then occurs more than four thousand times in the pages of Scripture that follow.

The VOICE again responded, without reluctance, without hesitation, and said,

> I AM WHO I AM; . . . THUS YOU SHALL SAY TO THE SONS OF ISRAEL, "I AM HAS SENT ME TO YOU. . . ." THUS YOU SHALL SAY TO THE SONS OF ISRAEL, "THE LORD, THE GOD OF YOUR FATHERS, THE GOD OF ABRAHAM, THE GOD OF ISAAC, AND THE GOD OF JACOB, HAS SENT ME TO YOU." THIS IS . . . MY MEMORIAL NAME TO ALL GENERATIONS. (Exodus 3:14, 15).

"I AM WHO I AM . . ." The name that is transliterated to read *Jehovah*, and appears throughout our Bible as LORD, spelled out in capital letters, was the name God gave to Moses.

It was His personal name.

It was to be remembered for all time.

To the sons of Israel, there was great reverence attached to this name. The people would not write it. They would not speak it. They would always substitute another like *Elohim* or *Adonai*. They would not speak the name *Jehovah* aloud.

In writing it they would use four Hebrew consonants—YHWH or YHUH. Or they would often just use four dashes to represent His name.

What does the name mean?

"I AM . . ." expresses the eternity of God.

Even Amun, the great god of Karnak, who had willed himself into being, had a beginning—but not Jehovah.

God has always been.

Before time was, God is.

After time ceases to exist, God is.

God *was* or God *shall be*, are inappropriate verb forms to use in the description of God.

God *is*.

> . . . from everlasting to everlasting, Thou art God" (Psalm 90:2).

Tozer writes:

> From the vanishing point to the vanishing point . . . The mind looks backward in time till the dim past vanishes and then turns and looks into the future till thought and imagination collapse from exhaustion, and God is at both points unaffected by either.[1]

The eternal God who knows neither beginning nor ending had just revealed to Moses that He was outside the boundaries of time and existed in the realm of forever.

> Time marks the beginning of created existence— but because God never began to exist, it can have no application to Him. [2]

The advanced age of Sarah, Abraham's wife, posed no problem to God when it was "time" for her to have a baby. Because time is of no consequence to God.

God lives in the timeless present—the everlasting NOW. With God there is no past—there is no future.

God dwells in eternity. Time dwells in God.

What a concept for a fearful Moses to grasp. If God is timeless, then God has already lived through all of our tomorrows, just as He has lived through all of our yesterdays.

God has already experienced the moment that I am experiencing right now.

In giving His name, He was telling Moses He already knew all that would happen when the time came to confront Pharaoh. God had already lived that moment.

Tomorrow comes as no threat or surprise to God. What a comfort that must have been to anxiety-prone Moses.

What a comfort that is to anxiety-prone me!

We measure time by a succession of events; by days, weeks, months, and years. We measure years by seasons.

As I write these words, summer is past, fall has begun. Winter is approaching. The chill is in the air, but some of the leaves still hang from the trees.

We are forced to wait through November for winter to begin and then through a long, dreary, endless winter, for spring to come.

God is not compelled to wait for anything. For God everything is present. Everything that will happen has already happened.

God is eternal—beyond the boundaries of time.

That's why God could look into the future and promise in Exodus 3:12 that Moses would return and worship at Mount Sinai.

That's why God knew how the sons of Israel would respond to Moses and in verse 18 could even quote their responses before they were spoken.

That's why God could describe the entire future scenario—the contest between Moses and Pharaoh as He did in verses 18-22, long before it even took place.

God is not prophesying. He is not making questionable predictions of future events. God is describing the future as He has already experienced it. He has been there.

"I AM . . ."

What a comfort to people like Moses who fear the future.

What a refuge for those of us who are obsessed and driven by time. "I AM . . ." That's His name—or at least part of it. There is more.

"I AM WHO I AM . . ."

The repetition is not for effect. It suggests that besides being eternal, God is self-existent.

God is independent—the only truly independent entity in the universe. He is not forced to depend upon any person or any thing for His existence.

God is self-contained—truly self-perpetuating. He

is not dependent upon the daylight to see or upon the sun to be warmed. He requires no food for sustenance, no rest for replenishment. He needs no outside source for wisdom or external force for strength.

He is self-existent.

He completely and totally sustains Himself.

He needs no help from anyone.

And if He needs no help from anyone . . . if He knows no limitations . . . if all that will ever be needed is already present in His Being, then He can be to Moses whatever Moses will ever need.

In giving His name to Moses, He is saying, "I am eternal, I will be to you whatever you need."

Notice that I did not say, "I will give you whatever you need."

In these five wonderful words that comprise His time-honored name, God is saying, "I will *be to you* whatever you need."

Moses could have said,

"But I will have needs."

God could have answered,

"But you will have Me."

Moses could have said,

"But I will need power."

God could have answered,

"But you will have Me."

Moses would have all the provision required for his great task, because he would have the Provider.

Psalm 23:1 takes the name Jehovah and beautifully illustrates its meaning. We read: "The Lord is my shepherd, I shall not want." Yet the passage could be read, "Since Jehovah is my Shepherd—I have everything I need."

Jesus took this eternal name and expanded it. (It is His name, too.) He stated some of our needs and then described Himself as the provision.

We need eternal life—

Jesus said, "I AM—the resurrection and the life. . . ." (John 11:25).

We need direction—

Jesus said, "I AM—the way. . . ." (John 14:6).

We need protection—

Jesus said, "I AM—the good shepherd. . . ." (John 10:14).

We need illumination—

Jesus said, "I AM—the light. . . ." (John 8:12).

We need access to heaven—

Jesus said, "I AM—the door. . . ." (John 10:9).

God was describing Himself to Moses and telling him that the God

who is different
who is gracious
who knows all
who is everywhere present and
who lives forever

would be the one Resource Person Moses could always depend upon.

God Himself would be the provision.

The Rev. R. I. Williams telephoned his sermon topic to the *Norfolk Ledger Dispatch.*

"The Lord is my Shepherd," he said.

"Is that all?" he was asked.

He replied, "That's enough."

The church page carried Mr. Williams' sermon topic as "The Lord is my Shepherd—that's enough."

That's what God was saying to Moses—He was enough. He was all that Moses would ever need.

He is all that we will ever need.

Chapter 13, Notes

1. A.W. Tozer, *The Knowledge of the Holy* (New York: Harper & Bros., 1961), p. 45.
2. Ibid.

**In God's wisdom there is no
guess or conjecture. He sees
everything in perfect focus.
Nothing is blurred. God sees
each event in proper relation
to all. He is able to proceed
toward predetermined goals
with flawless precision.**

CHAPTER FOURTEEN

(Exodus 3:15-22)

"Go and gather the elders. . . ."
(Exodus 3:16).

How in the world am I going to effect the release of two million hostages from Egypt's pharaoh?

I have no army.

I have no weapons.

I'm not even sure that I can convince the sons of Israel that they should leave!

Since God knew Moses' thoughts, He could answer before Moses ever questioned. In the instructions contained in verses 16 to 22, God lays out His strategy.

The problem of HOW was God's problem, not Moses'. God had made a promise and repeated it several times. It was time now to lay out His plan for moving an entire nation from one country to another.

At no other time in all of human history have so many moved so far—and all of them at one time—together.

Because God knows everything and can do anything—He could have bridged the gap of time and miraculously spoken a fleet of C 5-A Globemasters into existence. He could have sent down a host of angels to fly them. They could have transported two million refugees in one gigantic airlift across the tip of the Mediterranean and then parachuted them down to the top of the Mount of Olives.

Because God knows everything and can do anything—He could have "beamed" them all, like passengers in a futuristic space ship, from Goshen to Gilead.

Because God knows everything and can do anything—He could have swept them on angels' wings from Egypt to Canaan. But God had more at stake than just a massive withdrawal or resettlement campaign—more at stake than just the fulfillment of a promise.

His reputation was at stake. His personal integrity needed to be maintained. God was going to perform a miracle, but He was going to perform this miracle through real people. Real people who were going to make real decisions and take real action in the face of real and complex circumstances.

These people were going to have to be prepared people—prepared for any eventuality—any circumstance—in order that every element of the promise He'd made to Abraham could be fulfilled.

Moving the Hebrews from Point A to Point B was the least of his problems.

Follow the sovereign strategy of God as He works within the confines of the human will to get people to do what He wants them to do. Follow that strategy from the time He makes the promise to Abraham until He effects their release from Egypt.

Question: How can God enable one man, Abraham, to settle and dominate an entire region of the world already inhabited by seven hostile nations?

Answer: Move the descendants of that man into a compatible environment (Egypt) and then give them all the time they need to grow into a strong and powerful nation.

Question: How can God get them to move into that environment without coercion or force?

Answer: Allow a famine, which He did. Abraham's grandson Jacob and his twelve sons went to Egypt for no other reason—they thought—than to survive.

Question: How can God cause them to enter that land and not be suspicious aliens?

Answer: Send one of them in advance to infiltrate the government. God allowed this by sending Joseph, as a slave, and then causing his miraculous rise to power.

Question: How can the descendants of those twelve sons become numerous enough to have any significant influence anywhere?

Answer: Give them time—with no other pleasurable diversion in life than to have babies.

Question: How can God persuade this growing nation that has become settled, prosperous, and comfortable, to want to leave?

Answer: Place a paranoid king on the throne of Egypt—one who fears the rapid expansion of the alien Hebrews so much that he makes slaves out of them and even kills all of their boy babies.

Question: How can God strengthen the bodies of 600,000 men sufficiently to make them capable of surviving forced marches through unbearable heat, and then tough enough to engage in hand-to-hand conflict with hostile armies, and win?

Answer: Cause that paranoid king to be an egomaniac who wants to build treasure cities and fortresses and canals and walls. Have him send the slaves into brick yards to

> grub out the clay,
> carry the water,
> fetch the straw,
> build the molds,
> form the bricks,
> stack them,
> carry them, and then
> place them in position—

day after day in the blazing hot sun, with no respite and no relief.

What a body-building program!

Question: How can God deliver all these Hebrews in such a way as to make a lasting, favorable impression on an unbelieving world?

Answer: He can choose the least likely candidate to be their leader—a fugitive-killer who had been banished to the wilderness around Sinai. A shepherd who ought to be able to lead people since he had spent the last forty years leading stupid animals in his smelly, sweaty goat-skins in the impossible wilderness of Midian.

Question: How can God find a man with qualifications for such a task?

Answer: Cause that same man, before his banishment, to be adopted into the pharoah's family and then trained in the pharaoh's palace. Allow him to become second-in-command until he fully understands the mind of the pharaoh and the ways of all Egypt.

Question: How can God cause that same proud, arrogant prince to become obedient and submissive?

Answer: Allow that proud prince to fail and then to flee into the very desert where he will eventually lead the sons of Israel. Give him some irascible, dull-witted sheep and goats to work with until he learns to treat them with patience and gentleness.

Then give him a call—a divine call—an irrevocable call. Call this trained but broken man, give him all the resources he'll need, and then send him back to Egypt to show the world what Almighty God can accomplish through one prepared and willing servant.

That's what God did. And in so doing, God displayed His infinite, boundless, and perfect wisdom.

Paul says in Romans 11:33,

> Oh, the depth of the riches both of the wisdom and knowledge of God! How unsearchable are His judgments and unfathomable His ways!

God's wisdom is different from His omniscience.
Omniscience teaches us that God knows.
Wisdom teaches us that God *knows how*.

Wisdom is a moral as well as an intellectual quality. It is the inclination to choose the best and highest goal, with the surest means of attaining it.[1]

God's wisdom is something other than being

shrewd
cunning
smart
tricky
intelligent, or even
brilliant.

God's wisdom is His ability to choose perfect goals and then devise the surest means of reaching them.

God's wisdom allows Him to be the master strategist of space and time.

His wisdom was placed on obvious display in the strategy He employed in fulfilling His covenant promise to Abraham.

Most of us go through life

praying a little—
jockeying for position and power—
hoping, but never quite certain—
all the time secretly afraid that
we'll miss the best.

Not God! In God's wisdom there is no guess, no conjecture. He sees everything in clear focus. Nothing is blurred. God sees each event in proper relation to all others. He is able to proceed toward predetermined goals with flawless precision.

I toured the Amerock plant in Rockford, Illinois recently. It's there that precision hardware is manufactured from basic raw stock.

I heard the story of how G. W. Aldeen struggled for years to develop just the right process to give just the right appearance to a small cupboard hinge so that this brand new piece of hardware would have the appearance of an authentic antique.

How does one make something new look old?

How should it be buffed?

How many times?

With how much pressure?

With what sort of abrasive?

It took years to perfect that process. It became the envy of the industry.

God knew how to do that.

He didn't even have to think about it. God's wisdom is immediate and it's perfect.

God knows—that's omniscience.

And God knows how—that's wisdom.

Moses wanted to know how . . . God told him how.

God told him what to say.

> . . . THUS YOU SHALL SAY TO THE SONS OF IS-RAEL, "I AM HAS SENT ME TO YOU" (v. 14).

God told him how to proceed.

> GO AND GATHER THE ELDERS OF ISRAEL TO-GETHER, AND SAY TO THEM, "THE LORD, THE GOD OF YOUR FATHERS, THE GOD OF ABRAHAM, ISAAC AND JACOB, HAS APPEARED TO ME, SAY-ING, 'I AM INDEED CONCERNED ABOUT YOU AND WHAT HAS BEEN DONE TO YOU IN EGYPT. SO I SAID, I WILL BRING YOU UP OUT OF THE AFFLIC-TION OF EGYPT TO THE LAND OF THE CANAAN-ITE AND THE HITTITE AND THE AMORITE AND THE PERIZZITE AND THE HIVITE AND THE JEBU-SITE, TO A LAND FLOWING WITH MILK AND HONEY'" (vv. 16-17).

God told him how they would respond.

> AND THEY WILL PAY HEED TO WHAT YOU SAY; AND YOU WITH THE ELDERS OF ISRAEL WILL COME TO THE KING OF EGYPT . . . (v. 18).

God told him what to tell Pharaoh.

> . . . AND YOU WILL SAY TO HIM, "THE LORD, THE GOD OF THE HEBREWS, HAS MET WITH US. SO

NOW, PLEASE, LET US GO A THREE DAYS' JOUR-
NEY INTO THE WILDERNESS, THAT WE MAY SAC-
RIFICE TO THE LORD OUR GOD" (v. 18).

God told him just how Pharaoh would respond.

BUT I KNOW THAT THE KING OF EGYPT WILL NOT
PERMIT YOU TO GO, EXCEPT UNDER COMPUL-
SION (v. 19).

God told Moses what He would do.

SO I WILL STRETCH OUT MY HAND, AND STRIKE
EGYPT WITH ALL MY MIRACLES WHICH I SHALL
DO IN THE MIDST OF IT. . . ." (v. 20)

God told him what Pharaoh would then do.

. . . AND AFTER THAT HE WILL LET YOU GO. . . .
(v. 20).

God told him what He would do to the Egyptians.

AND I WILL GRANT THIS PEOPLE FAVOR IN THE
SIGHT OF THE EGYPTIANS. . . . (v. 21).

God told him what the Egyptians would do for
Israel.

. . . AND IT SHALL BE THAT WHEN YOU GO, YOU
WILL NOT GO EMPTY-HANDED. BUT EVERY
WOMAN SHALL ASK OF HER NEIGHBOR AND THE
WOMAN WHO LIVES IN HER HOUSE, ARTICLES OF
SILVER AND ARTICLES OF GOLD, AND CLOTHING;
AND YOU WILL PUT THEM ON YOUR SONS AND
DAUGHTERS. THUS YOU WILL PLUNDER THE
EGYPTIANS (vv. 21-22).

Any enemy of God is at a distinct disadvantage.
There is no element of uncertainty, whatever, when you
follow the all-wise counsel and strategy of a God who has
already lived through the contest that you're presently
planning.

That's God's wisdom. God knows how to get His
people from Point A to Point B. He is the master strategist
of all time.

God has a predetermined goal for every believer. It is clearly stated in Romans 8:29. In His wisdom He has planned to ultimately "conform [us all] to the image of His Son, [Jesus Christ]." His changeless goal is to make us all like Jesus.

God's goal for us is not a trouble-free life or a prosperous existence. God's goal is transformation—change from the basic raw product to an attractive, desirable, and irresistible lifestyle that will be transferred from ourselves to others.

Change takes time. It takes buffing. It requires abrasives. God's wisdom has set the best and most perfect goal. He knows just what it takes to get us there.

Moses could never have accomplished what God wanted unless he had first come to know what He really had in mind for him and for the Hebrew slaves in Egypt.

And the wisdom that was available to Moses is available to us all. It's not really difficult to appropriate. James has made it sound quite simple, actually. He tells us in chapter one, verse five, that all we have to do is ask for it. That's all—just ask for it.

That's hard for some of us who already think we know it all, but easy for those of us who have learned from bitter experience, like Moses, that we really need the pure, peaceable kind of wisdom that only comes from God.

Chapter 14, Notes

1. J. I. Packer, *Knowing God* (Downers Grove, Ill.: InterVarsity Press, 1973), p. 80.

**Mercy costs something.
Sympathy can be free.
Compassion can even be
cheap, but mercy costs
something.**

CHAPTER FIFTEEN

(Exodus 3:16, 17)

"I am indeed concerned about you. . . ."
(Exodus 3:16).

A small boy had been out riding his bicycle. He arrived home later than expected. His mother asked, "Why are you so late?"

"Billy's bike broke and I've been helping him fix it," the boy answered.

"How in the world could you help Billy fix his bicycle? You're only six years old! You don't know how to repair a bicycle."

"I know," said Billy, "but I was helping him anyway."

"What in the world did you do to help him?"

"Well, when Billy's bike broke, he sat down on the curb to cry—so I sat down to cry with him."

In Exodus, chapter 3, we have listened as God spoke from the midst of a flaming tree to Moses about two million Hebrew prisoners. A nation of slaves who sat alongside the curbs of Egypt—crying because their world had collapsed—their lives had ended.

Their days were being spent in burdensome labor. Their numbers were being decimated by back-breaking toil. Their sons were being thrown to the crocodiles along the banks of the River Nile.

They were refused the privilege of worshiping their God. They were in deep grief and constant fear.

Nothing soothed them.

Nothing relieved them.

They lived in the silent sorrow of unending, unbearable grief.

Like a six-year-old boy whose bicycle has just broken, their whole world seemed to be coming to an end—and they didn't know how to fix it.

In the midst of detailed instructions as to what Moses was to do, Jehovah paused to express His sympathy. God sat down beside them to cry.

The VOICE said,

> GO AND GATHER THE ELDERS OF ISRAEL TOGETHER, AND SAY TO THEM, "THE LORD, THE GOD OF YOUR FATHERS, THE GOD OF ABRAHAM, ISAAC AND JACOB, HAS APPEARED TO ME, SAYING, 'I AM INDEED CONCERNED ABOUT YOU AND WHAT HAS BEEN DONE TO YOU IN EGYPT. . . .'" (v. 16).

"I am indeed concerned about you. . . ."

In those six words, God opened His heart to a weary people and shared with them His compassion,

His care,

His concern.

Now, God was about to display His mercy.

Dr. A. W. Tozer has said in one of His magnificent prayers,

> O Father God,
> Thy wisdom excites our admiration—
> Thy power fills us with fear—
> Thy omnipresence turns every spot into holy ground.
> But how shall we thank Thee for Thy mercy?

Thy mercy which comes down to the lowest part
of our need
To give us beauty for ashes—
The oil of joy for mourning—
And for the spirit of heaviness—
The garment of praise.

Tozer went on to say,

We shall have a thousand strings to play on our
harps, but the sweetest may well be the one tuned
to sound forth the mercy of God.

The words, "indeed concerned" do not define the
word *mercy*.

Concern has more in common with the word *compassion* than it does with the word *mercy*. *Mercy* does find its
roots, its beginnings, its stirrings, however, in the word
concern.

Concern, like *compassion*, is a feeling word.

The little boy who sat on the curb alongside his broken-hearted friend was feeling something. He was feeling sorry for his companion. He was experiencing concern for his friend.

He was feeling sorrow by sitting down to cry.

He was displaying compassion.

He was doing the one and only thing he could do in
the face of his friend's tragedy. He was performing that
one act of love that each of us needs when we're hurting.

When I was hospitalized for depression, the callers I
appreciated most were those who offered no solutions,
prescribed no remedies, and delivered no sermons. The
ones who penetrated my lonely and baffling world
prayed no prayers and offered no Scripture. They just sat
down with me and cried.

They didn't pretend to know the cause.

They certainly didn't offer any solutions.

Two words repeatedly pulled back the heavy curtain
of emptiness. Those words were, "I'm sorry." Those two
words, spoken in love, said it all—all I could handle and

all that I seemed to need to hear. "I'm sorry . . . I'm sorry."

Through Moses, God was about to deliver those two words to His hurting Hebrew family.

God was concerned.
He heard their cries.
He was aware of their groanings.
He had seen their suffering.
He had witnessed their beatings.
He had felt the pain of the whips.

And He hurt. He hurt for them. He hurt with them.

That's what God meant when He said, "I am indeed concerned about you and what has been done to you in Egypt."

It's always comforting to know that someone, somewhere, understands what's happening and how you feel.

When I wrote the book *Depression*, I had no intention of unraveling the complex problem of major depressive illness. What I really wanted to do was to let those in the black hole of depression know that there was someone who really knew how that felt.

God knew how the Hebrews felt. That's insight.

He entered into their pain with them. That's empathy.

He told them He was sorry. That's compassion.

But neither insight, empathy, nor even compassion are to be confused with mercy. When we talk about the New Testament spiritual gift of mercy, we often confuse it with compassion. We assume that because one is empathetic, concerned, and genuinely sorry, that person has the gift of mercy.

Mercy is more than insight.
Mercy is more than empathy.
Mercy is more than compassion.
Mercy is compassion plus action.

Mercy sees a problem, feels deeply about that problem, and then moves with the ability to correct that problem.

When read together, verses 16 and 17 of chapter 3 beautifully illustrate mercy. The VOICE said,

> . . . I AM INDEED CONCERNED ABOUT YOU AND WHAT HAS BEEN DONE TO YOU IN EGYPT. SO I SAID, "I WILL BRING YOU UP OUT OF THE AFFLICTION OF EGYPT TO THE LAND OF THE CANAANITE AND THE HITTITE AND THE AMORITE AND THE PERIZZITE AND THE HIVITE AND THE JEBUSITE, TO A LAND FLOWING WITH MILK AND HONEY."

Mercy is not only sharing the pain—mercy is sharing the pain and then relieving it.

I once visited a dear friend who had just undergone a kidney transplant. When I walked into his hospital room, I found him standing by the window hooked up to numerous tubes and monitors. As he greeted me, I noticed he was trying to hide a recurring and terribly distressing pain.

He had the hiccups. He'd had them for two days. He was exhausted from the pain that strained at the sutures and stressed the wounds that had been made to his body.

His roommates occasionally laughed—with nervous humor. I laughed—at first—until I realized the severity of the problem.

I visited with him, rejoiced with him over the success of the surgery, read to him, and then told him how sorry I was for the recurring pain over which neither the doctors nor his medication seemed to have any control.

I prayed with him.

I thanked God for the new kidney made available by some anonymous donor, for the successful surgery, for the return of energy, and then asked God for complete recovery.

As I was about to leave, I put my arm on my friend's shoulder, told him that I'd continue to pray, and then asked, "Is there anything else I can do for you?"

Without a moment's hesitation he said, "Yes, Pastor, you can pray that my hiccups will stop."

I was somewhat stunned by his request—embarrassed even, that I had neglected to mention the obvious need. At the same time I must admit to feeling somewhat cornered. I was being asked to specifically pray for relief for an obvious problem in front of a group of skeptical observers, with the full realization that in only a few seconds' time everyone would know whether or not that prayer had been answered.

Without a word, I took his hand in mine and said, "And Father, we ask You in Jesus' name to relieve Erwin of these hiccups. Amen."

As soon as I said, "Amen," the room fell strangely and completely silent. Not one of the three roommates stirred. Two incoming visitors stopped at the door and waited. An orderly stood quietly with medication in hand in the middle of the room.

For a brief, frightening moment, I wanted to disappear. I stood motionless and waited.

All eyes were focused on Erwin.

All ears strained, listening for that aggravating spasm to recur. Nothing happened. The seconds ticked by. A minute passed—two minutes—and then with an overwhelming sense of relief, Erwin's face broke into a wide grin.

I casually said, "Thank You, Father."

The roommates applauded. One of them said, "Good show, preacher, let's see you do that one again."

I left quickly—thankfully.

Erwin relaxed.

The hiccups never returned.

Compassion, concern, and empathy were all in evidence during my visit. And yet, *mercy* was not displayed until I took the instrument of prayer and employed it to relieve the problem.

Mercy means to feel pity. It means to display compassion. It means to enter actively into the pain of another—to weep when others weep. But it means even more than that.

Mercy not only feels badly about the condition of another, it *moves* with the wisdom and the ability to correct the problem.

When God says,

> "I am indeed concerned about you"
>   and
> "I will bring you up out of the affliction,"

He is displaying His mercy.

Mercy is active compassion.

It is compassion made visible.

It is compassion that relieves and delivers.

It is concern that has the capacity to change circumstances, relieve pressure, and remove problems.

> Mercy is that inexhaustible energy within the divine nature which predisposes God to be actively compassionate.[1]

But it's more.

Dr. A. H. Strong says,

> Mercy is the eternal principle of God's nature which leads Him to seek the temporal good and eternal salvation of those who oppose themselves to His will, even at the cost of infinite self-sacrifice.[2]

Mercy costs something.

Sympathy can be free.

Compassion can even be cheap, but mercy costs something.

Moses knew little about mercy. Mercy was not an attribute of the multiple gods of Egypt. The false gods of Egypt were quick to punish whenever they were offended.

Picture a scene such as the following.

On one of his visits to the magnificent palace of Apis the sacred bull, near the city of Memphis, Moses was ascending the broad steps when he became aware of a great commotion nearby. He stopped to watch an irate crowd of offended citizens chase a seaman from Tyre across the temple square.

The fugitive was pale as a corpse and running as fast as possible. He fell at the feet of Egypt's prince and begged Moses for mercy.

"What have you done?" asked Moses.

"The wheel of my chariot accidentally ran over the body of a small cat and killed it, sire," he answered.

"I'm sorry," said Moses. (That was compassion.)

"There is nothing I can do. You have killed one of Egypt's sacred animals."

With that the crowd rushed the offender away, threw him to the ground, trampled him until he was a shapeless mass and then divided his remains among the crowd to be fed to the sacred cats that were kept inside the temple. (That was justice.)

Moses knew much about the justice of the gods of Egypt.

He was a shepherd in Midian for forty years because of justice.

He was deposed because of justice.

He was a fugitive because of justice.

The sentence of death hung over his head because of justice.

Mercy tempers justice.

Mercy restrains justice.

Mercy takes the full weight of justice upon itself to prevent punishment.

Mercy is that act of God which intervenes in a manner perfectly consistent with all that God is. It releases the guilty from the penalty and bondage of his sin solely on the basis of the sacrificial death of Jesus Christ on the cross.

It is love, compassion, concern, and a sympathy that is activated by a divine energy that empowers it to do more than feel. It empowers feeling to be translated into action.

Compassion could have only showered sympathy

on the suffering Hebrews. Mercy delivered them.

Compassion can accompany man to hell, but only mercy can deliver him from hell.

King David knew God's mercy.

Justice required the death penalty for the great sins that David committed. Mercy acknowledged the severity of those sins, the reality of those sins, and the offended holiness of a just and righteous God, and then moved in forgiveness in response to the confession of the penitent monarch.

For the rest of his life David sang of the mercies of the Lord. God's hand of mercy stays God's hand of justice without in any way compromising God's unalterable righteousness.

One of the pieces of furniture constructed by Moses during the building of the Tabernacle was called "the ark" —the ark of the covenant.

It was just a box made of acacia wood. It was 3 1/2 feet long and 27 inches wide—just about the size of an old Government Issue foot locker.

Moses had been instructed to place the Decalogue, or "Ten Commandments," inside the ark. The laws contained in the box pronounced every person guilty of offending a holy God. Every person deserved justice. Every person was under the sentence of death.

When the box was completed and the law was in place, God then instructed Moses to build a lid for the box.

The lid was 3 1/2 feet long and 27 inches wide—just the right size to cover the box completely.

The cover was overlaid with pure gold and topped with two angelic beings at either end.

The lid that covered the box containing the laws that had already been broken was called the Mercy Seat.

It was there that

    the hand of justice was stayed
      the power of justice was limited and
        the penalty of justice was satisfied.

It was there that God's just demands were satisfied by His own merciful provision.

God's concern for the sufferers of Egypt combined with His mercy to design a provision for His broken laws and His offended holiness.

His deliverance was to be made possible by a sacrificial offering that satisfied His justice, and made possible a merciful and miraculous deliverance from centuries of endless bondage.

God was concerned.

He hurt deeply, but then . . . He *acted* to deliver the prisoner and set him free.

Chapter 15, Notes

1. A. W. Tozer, *The Knowledge of the Holy* (New York: Harper & Bros., 1961), p. 96.
2. A. H. Strong, *Systematic Theology* (Philadelphia: Judson Press, 1907), p. 289.

**God has all the power needed
to do all that He wishes to do.
His power is found in
undiminished fullness in His
own limitless Being.**

CHAPTER SIXTEEN

(Exodus 4:1-9)

"What is that in your hand?" (Exodus 4:2).

God was unwrapping the cloak of mystery that had enshrouded Him for so long. He was peeling off layer after layer of divine truth in a process of self-disclosure designed to prepare Moses for the most demanding assignment of his lifetime.

Through the flaming tree God spoke and revealed attributes to Moses He had disclosed to no one.

God had outlined His strategy and revealed all the resources that were being placed at Moses' disposal.

But Moses was not convinced that God's strategy and God's resources were adequate. He asked,

> What if they will not believe me, or listen to what I say? For they may say, "The Lord has not appeared to you" (Exodus 4:1).

The VOICE answered,

WHAT IS THAT IN YOUR HAND?

"A staff," Moses replied.

Just a stick, really. A walking stick. A cracked and gnarled acacia tree. Moses used it as a staff to aid him in picking his way over the boulders and climbing the steep sides of the mountain walls. It came in handy when the animals needed some gentle prodding.

Walking sticks were common in Egypt. The gods all carried staffs or rods. Ptah, Bast, Amon Re and Hathor are all pictured with walking sticks. Of course, theirs were not of wood—but of gold.

The VOICE spoke again,

THROW IT DOWN.

Moses obeyed. There was no reluctance—no hesitancy. The awesomeness of the flaming spectacle in front of him, and the authority of the commands made him immediately compliant.

The moment the staff hit the ground it turned into a hissing, frightening snake. It coiled and recoiled, its eyes straying from the form of the tall man that stood paralyzed with fright.

Although black cobras were a common sight in both Egypt and Sinai, they were highly respected. One learned to keep at a safe distance.

Moses was too close. He fled from the snake.

I hate snakes. In Africa we were constantly on the lookout for spitting cobras.

In New Guinea, I stumbled onto a fifteen-foot python. I was carrying an old Thompson submachine gun that held a drum containing fifty bullets.

I shot the python—fifty times.

Cobras were a sign of power and protection in Egypt. They were included as a part of the dress of the pharaoh. The head of the cobra was carved of gold and worn as part of the king's headgear.

They were also placed in burial chambers to discourage grave robbers. They caused fear to all who came near, and represented power to all who displayed them. Their presence suggested that no one dare approach or question the authority of the rulers of Egypt. The leaders were invulnerable—protected and safe.

God revealed to Moses His power—His all-powerfulness in all of earth's kingdoms. His ability to change the staff—a member of the vegetable kingdom—into a snake—a member of the animal kingdom—was a visible demonstration of omnipotence.

The VOICE spoke again,

> STRETCH OUT YOUR HAND AND GRASP IT BY ITS TAIL.

People never pick up live, venomous snakes by the tail. I have a picture of my wife, Martha, holding a cobra by the tail, but it was dead.

Moses looked around for a forked stick, a piece of cloth—anything to render the serpent harmless. Yet the voice had said to stretch out his *hand*—to grasp the serpent by the *tail*. Moses S T R E T C H E D. He reached as far away from his body as possible. If he had to be bitten, he would much rather it be on the hand than the face.

What happened? The nightmarish snake became a harmless stick of wood the moment Moses' finger touched it.

It was so appropriate for God to use a cobra. Moses knew of its awesome place of power in the land of Egypt.

It was so considerate of God to give Moses that display of His power.

God is fearful of no one—no thing. He is all-powerful, omnipotent, almighty.

God has all the power that is needed to do all that He wishes to do. His power lies in undiminished fullness in His own limitless Being.

The VOICE spoke again,

> THAT THEY MAY BELIEVE THAT THE LORD, THE GOD OF THEIR FATHERS, THE GOD OF ABRAHAM, THE GOD OF ISAAC, AND THE GOD OF JACOB, HAS APPEARED TO YOU.

The staff and the snake became a sign to convince an unconvinced people, and they later became a warning to Pharaoh and his magicians that God was greater than the snake god of Egypt.

Again the VOICE spoke,

NOW PUT YOUR HAND INTO YOUR BOSOM.

Moses obeyed. He reached his hand into the folds of his robe and felt the skin of his chest. When he pulled it out, his hand was leprous—white as new-fallen snow.

Leprosy at this stage was hideous to look at. And it was terminal. There was no cure. The symptoms were loathsome. The victim was an outcast. Death was the only hope of relief.

Moses was repulsed by the sight. He couldn't believe that he had advanced through all the stages of leprosy in just one moment of time.

To Moses, leprosy meant that all contact with Zipporah his wife, Jethro his father-in-law, and his two sons, had to cease immediately. The fugitive outcast had become an untouchable until . . .

The VOICE said,

PUT YOUR HAND INTO YOUR BOSOM AGAIN.

Moses did as he was told—more quickly this time. When he took his hand out again, it was restored like the rest of his flesh.

It was as though Moses had been given back his life. The terminal illness was not simply arrested. It had not gone into remission—it was *gone*. He was totally healed.

The VOICE spoke again,

AND IT SHALL COME ABOUT THAT IF THEY WILL NOT BELIEVE YOU OR HEED THE WITNESS OF THE FIRST SIGN, THEY MAY BELIEVE THE WITNESS OF THE LAST SIGN.

BUT IT SHALL BE THAT IF THEY WILL NOT BELIEVE EVEN THESE TWO SIGNS OR HEED WHAT YOU SAY, THEN YOU SHALL TAKE SOME WATER FROM THE NILE AND POUR IT ON THE DRY GROUND; AND THE WATER WHICH YOU TAKE FROM THE NILE WILL BECOME BLOOD ON THE DRY GROUND.

God's display of power is complete. All the kingdoms of earth are subject to Him.

> The animal kingdom,
>> the vegetable kingdom,
>>> the mineral kingdom—

even the spiritual kingdom, for the serpent is always a representation of Satan.

The word *almighty* is used fifty-six times in Scripture. It is never used of anyone but God.

He alone is almighty.

Only God is all-powerful.

> God has an incomprehensible plenitude of power—a potency that is absolute. Since God is infinite, His power is without limit. God has unlimited power. God has the power to do all things which are objects of His power, with or without means.[1]

God could have spoken a serpent into being without a staff, and a staff into being without a serpent. That's omnipotence!

God can do anything as easily as He can do anything else.

I can press one hundred pounds, but I can't press one thousand pounds.

I can't press one hundred pounds as easily as I can press fifty pounds.

But God can do anything as easily as He can do anything else. The weight of an object is of no concern to God.

God is all-powerful.

All of His acts are done without effort.

God expends energy without depleting it.

God expends energy without becoming tired.

God never perspires—is never out of breath. He never requires rest. He never sleeps.

All of His acts are done without effort.

God is all-powerful.

Everything in the heavens above remains in place because God tells it to. He, in the person of His Son, "upholds all things by the word of His power" (Hebrews 1:3).

This galaxy of ours with its 100 billion stars, of which only two thousand are visible on a clear night, is only one of a billion other galaxies. It is estimated that in addition to the billion universes we can see, there are other billions beyond our sight, and even beyond our comprehension.

In the Book of Hebrews we are told that He upholds it all by just a word—an effortless command—maybe even just a whisper.

God doesn't even have to snap His finger—just a word will do it.

God is all-powerful.

He holds the whole world in His hand.

He holds the little tiny baby in His hand.

He holds you and me, brother, in His hand.

My major depressive illness limited me for four years. I resigned my pastorate and was told that my ministry was finished.

God displayed His all-powerfulness to me—in a moment—while on my knees. The cloud lifted. The depression left. The blackness dispersed, and it has never returned.

The all-powerful God declared to Moses—and to us—that all the lesser powers of earth and time are subject to the greater power of our God.

God was preparing Moses for the inevitable moment when heaven's power, operating through a submissive and responsive person, would collide with earth's power represented by an arrogant and mighty monarch.

God was showing Moses, in advance, who would win.

Chapter 16, Notes

1. A. H. Strong, *Systematic Theology* (Philadelphia: Judson Press, 1907), p 289

It was not God that worried Moses, it was Moses.

CHAPTER SEVENTEEN

(Exodus 4:10-13)

"Who has made man's mouth?" (Exodus 4:11).

When Kathy was small, she climbed on my lap, looked at my face, and then began tracing my features with her finger.

She ran her finger over my eyebrows and then down the bridge of my nose. She lightly touched each eye and brushed along their lashes. She outlined my cheeks, felt my lips and then ran her finger down over my chin.

"What are you doing?" I asked.

"Just studying you," she answered.

Moses was studying God—tracing His nature, His attributes, His very being through the presence of the flaming tree. He was listening to the VOICE—the VOICE of the living God as He revealed Himself to this son of Israel.

Moses had heard every word. His attention never wavered even though his faith did. He still wasn't convinced that God was able to use him. It wasn't God that worried Moses. It was Moses.

He still didn't feel qualified or adequate.

I have long since learned that if I wait until I feel

qualified or adequate, I will never do anything. I always feel unqualified and inadequate.

Moses, like most of us, was looking at his own weakness rather than God's strength.

He said,

> Please, Lord, I have never been eloquent, neither recently nor in time past, nor since Thou hast spoken to Thy servant; for I am slow of speech and slow of tongue (Exodus 4:10).

Moses had a speech problem.

We don't know whether Moses had an actual impediment or not. Some believe he stuttered. Others say he had difficulty pronouncing the labials, b - m - p - and w.

Some think he stammered.

Moses said that he was just "slow of speech." He felt there was too much lag time between his brain and his tongue. It took more time than he felt was necessary to find the appropriate words.

He was slow in his speech

> like Martin Luther,
>   John Knox, and
>   Oliver Cromwell.
> Like the apostle Paul.

Moses lacked confidence—in his speech—in his ability—in himself—like most of us.

Moses lacked self-esteem, struggled with a poor self-concept, a weak self-image—like most of us.

The VOICE responded to Moses with some baffling words,

> WHO HAS MADE MAN'S MOUTH? OR WHO MAKES HIM DUMB OR DEAF, OR SEEING OR BLIND? IS IT NOT I, THE LORD? (Exodus 4:11).

God was reminding Moses of His power—His creative power.

But when He asked the question, "WHO MAKES MAN DUMB OR DEAF OR SEEING OR BLIND?" and then added, "IS IT NOT I, THE LORD?" He was opening the curtain to reveal the staggering truth of His sovereignty.

We struggle with this question. We are quick to give Him credit for all the good that happens, but here He is taking credit for the bad as well. In this remarkable declaration He claimed that He was the One finally and ultimately responsible for everything—even a personal inability to speak and to hear and to see.

God was assuming full and final responsibility for all that happens—

> in this world, and
> in this life.

That's what is meant by the word *sovereignty*. Sovereignty is the activity of God's authority—His control—His supremacy in command of everything.

Sovereignty is God's rule and overrule over everything.

We speak of sovereignty when we glibly say, "God is still on the throne."

We mean,

> God is in control,
> He rules,
> He is King, or
> He is Sovereign.

God's sovereignty is in evidence repeatedly in Exodus, chapters 3 and 4.

When God said in chapter 4, verse 21, that He would harden Pharaoh's heart, He was claiming sovereignty or control over a person's heart.

When God said that He would strike Egypt with all His miracles, in chapter 3, verse 20, He was claiming sovereignty or control over the physical world.

When He stated in that same verse that He would cause Pharaoh to change his mind and release the Hebrews, He was claiming sovereignty or control even over the will of man.

God is either king over all or He is not king at all.

God rules His entire creation.

That's a difficult thought for all of us. The implications of sovereignty lead us down dark alleys of confusion that seem to have no outlet. Yes, this is a bewildering truth. Yet that does not make it any less true.

Only God can be sovereign. God's omnipresence enables God's sovereignty. If there were but one place He could not be, He would not be sovereign.

Only God can be sovereign. God's omnipotence enables God's sovereignty. If there were but one thing He could not do, He would not be sovereign.

Only God can be sovereign. God's omniscience enables God's sovereignty. If there were but one thing He could not know, He would not be sovereign.

Sovereignty implies freedom.

God is free to do whatever He wills to do—

> anywhere
> anytime
> without any explanation!

No one, no thing enjoys absolute freedom but God.

> No one can stop Him.
> Nothing can hinder Him or compel Him.
> He is able to do as He pleases.
> He possesses universal authority.
> He needs ask permission of no one.[1]

God is sovereign because God is in control. God is in control because God is sovereign. He can make man dumb or blind or seeing. He can give permission to Satan to devastate Job. He can do as He pleases, and as in Job's case, He owes no one an explanation.

He can choose an Isaac and not an Ishmael,

> a Jacob and not an Esau,
> a Jew and not a Gentile,

and He owes no one an explanation.

Why? Because He's God, and He has the right—the knowledge —the wisdom—the grace—the authority—the freedom and the power to do as He pleases.

He can give permission for

> crops to fail,
> business to falter,
> children to die,
> health to deteriorate,
> friends to desert, and
> life to collapse,

as He did with Job.

He can cause

> prosperity,
> good health,
> great wealth,
> abounding happiness, and
> security

to those who seem least to deserve it—and He owes no explanations.

The Lord causes the sun to rise and the sun to set. If He wanted it to stand still—He could do that too, and He has.

God is free to act

> when He pleases,
> where He pleases,
> as He pleases,

and is only limited by a nature that forbids inconsistency with itself.

Sovereignty is filled with surprises.

Who would think that bland, uninteresting words like—

> Now Moses was pasturing the flock of Jethro, his father-in-law . . .

would provide the backdrop for one of the most dramatic sagas of all of human history?

Who would think that God would reach across miles of barren desert to tap an obscure shepherd to lead two million Hebrews out of bondage? Man seldom chooses a failure when he is seeking a warrior, but that's what a sovereign God did.

Moses seemed like a most unlikely candidate for giving a code of laws to the world. He had already broken most of them.

It would never have occurred to me to look *to* Egypt's throne to find deliverance *from* Egypt's throne.

I would never have thought to seek release from the nearly limitless power of Egypt's pharaoh from the direction of Egypt's pharaoh-elect.

Who would have thought that the God of heaven would have selected a god of earth to reveal Him?

That's almost as incredible as the Church of Jesus Christ growing at its most rapid pace when led by the apostle Paul—the church's former persecutor.

God is full of surprises, isn't He?

I doubt that I would have given any meaning to Moses' flight from Egypt. Sovereignty controlled it completely. Moses fled in the very direction and through the same wilderness, and to the same location He would lead the Hebrews forty years later.

Sovereignty allows God to be God. It allows Him the freedom to do what man oftentimes believes unthinkable.

God had sovereignly allowed Moses' speech patterns, and God implied that He would and could make correction. That was not a problem too big for God. He could cause Moses to speak with an eloquence equivalent to His own.

This was too much for Moses to comprehend or to believe. Moses asked God to send somebody else.

> Please, Lord, now send the message by whomever Thou wilt (v. 13).

This was too much for God. God sovereignly pushed Moses partially back into his prison house of unbelief and sovereignly chose to use Aaron to be his spokesman for the rest of his life.

The VOICE from within the flames rose in anger against Moses:

> IS THERE NOT YOUR BROTHER AARON THE LEVITE? I KNOW THAT HE SPEAKS FLUENTLY. . . . YOU ARE TO SPEAK TO HIM AND PUT THE WORDS IN HIS MOUTH; AND I, EVEN I, WILL BE WITH YOUR MOUTH AND HIS MOUTH, AND I WILL TEACH YOU WHAT YOU ARE TO DO. MOREOVER, HE SHALL SPEAK FOR YOU TO THE PEOPLE; AND IT SHALL BE THAT HE SHALL BE AS A MOUTH FOR YOU, AND YOU SHALL BE AS GOD TO HIM (Exodus 4:14-16).

God had sovereignly spoken and sovereignly acted and sovereignly rejected Moses for the task of being His spokesman. He could lead the people, but he was to be permanently impaired with a speech defect that would embarrass him every time he opened his mouth.

He was handicapped, and limited by his own unbelief. When I read the story of Moses, I see the fall of one of earth's mightiest from the pinnacle of fame to the humiliation and shame of forty years of complete obscurity, and then I see him begin a second forty years with a humiliating limitation.

He hardly seems to me to be a worthy candidate for becoming the friend of God, the champion of Israel and the forger of the nation that will ultimately rule the world.

But a sovereign God sees differently. He sees all, knows all, and can do all. A sovereign God acts as only sovereignty wills to act, even to the point of taking a limited faith and a limited ability in a limited man, and exalting him above all others.

God does as He pleases,

> when He pleases,
> where He pleases,
> how He pleases, and
> with whom He pleases.

And that's a very comforting truth to me. That means that God can use even a person like me—or even a person like you—if He chooses, and nothing, not even the mightiest forces on earth, can interfere with that plan.

First Samuel 2:6-8 proclaims the sovereignty of God as fully and completely as it can ever be proclaimed.

> The Lord kills and makes alive;
> He brings down to Sheol and raises up.
> The Lord makes poor and rich;
> He brings low, He also exalts.
> He raises the poor from the dust,
> He lifts the needy from the ash heap
> To make them sit with nobles,
> And inherit a seat of honor;
> For the pillars of the earth are the LORD'S,
> And He set the world on them.

The alternatives to God being sovereign are frightening.

If God isn't in control, then who is?

> Is Satan?
> Is man?
> Are you?
> Is no one?

The alternatives are disturbing, aren't they? Take heart, though. God is in control. He's still on the throne. He always will be.

No one can ever take Him down.

Chapter 17, Notes

1. A. W. Tozer, *The Knowledge of the Holy* (New York: Harper & Bros., 1961), p. 116.

Moses, armed with a gnarled and crooked piece of wood for a staff, and assisted by a fellow Hebrew named Aaron, began waging his war on the mightiest force in the known world. . . .

CHAPTER EIGHTEEN

(Exodus 4:14—12:51)

"Let My people go. . . ." (Exodus 5:1).

Two men approached the palace of the pharaoh. One was dressed in the goat skins of a shepherd, the other in the rags of a slave.

Both walked tall and erect.

Both were frightened.

Their request for an audience with the king had been first ignored and then delayed. It was finally granted—more out of curiosity than obligation.

Amenhotep II, high potentate of all Egypt, the pharaoh of the land of the pyramids, the reigning god of earth, was really interested only in the story of a deposed prince.

Since Thutmose III had died, there'd been little concern for finding and killing the fugitive. The oppressive load of labor, the pains of servitude, and the pressures of persecution upon the sons of Israel had increased severely. Moses had been all but forgotten.

Moses and Aaron were led past the wondrous temple of the sun, surrounded by lakes that looked like mirrored glass. Not a single ripple disturbed the reflection of the two obelisks that stood along their shores.

They walked up a long flight of broad steps where a hundred Theban soldiers stood like statues, each holding a spear.

Doors, decorated with shaved ivory and inlaid with emeralds, opened into a chamber surrounded by columns ninety feet high. A wide aisle, lined by statues of the gods and a brilliant array of army officers in dazzling uniforms, led to the king's throne.

The strange entourage of two ragged ambassadors was escorted to a spot between the gods Osiris and Isis. They bowed low before Amenhotep, who sat on a throne that rested upon the bodies of two lion-leopards made from Rhodian marble. The throne was shaded with an expanded canopy of feathers—all of ivory, yet so delicately carved that they waved in the slight breeze that stirred in the colossal hall.

This was the throne that once beckoned to Moses. This was where he would have sat to rule the world. Now it was occupied by an arrogant, vicious, uncaring pagan who wondered what could possibly be so important as to have caused these two strange men to have petitioned the king persistently for an audience.

Amenhotep motioned for them to rise and permitted them to speak.

Moses turned to Aaron and slowly began to put words alongside each other—words that had been prompted by God. With freedom and fluency, Aaron then passed them on to the king.

The pharaoh watched the human spectacle before him. He looked at the long hair, the beard, the clothes of the man called Moses. He watched and waited for the halting words that came from the lips of the former prince.

"Can this be Moses?" he thought. "Is this the man who aspired to the throne—the man who commanded Egypt's armies and conquered surrounding nations?"

Amenhotep could scarcely believe the message his eyes were conveying. He believed it even less when he heard the demands that came from these two old Hebrews.

> Thus says the Lord, the God of Israel, "Let My people go that they may celebrate a feast to Me in the wilderness" (Exodus 5:1).

The words fell from Aaron's lips like exploding shells. Those were the first words that signified the beginning of the mighty contest which was about to take place.

Pharaoh's response was to laugh—the cynical laugh of arrogance—and ask,

> Who is the Lord that I should obey His voice to let Israel go? I do not know the Lord, and besides, I will not let Israel go" (v. 2).

Moses and Aaron continued to make their demands of Amenhotep. The king refused. He tightened his grip on the sons of Israel and increased the pressures upon the slaves.

Moses, armed only with a gnarled and crooked piece of wood for a staff and assisted by a fellow-Hebrew, his brother Aaron, began waging his war on the mightiest force in the known world—a war that ultimately left the magnificent throne vacant, the pharaoh dead, all of Egypt in mourning, and the Hebrew slaves free.

After repeated refusals, Pharaoh began to feel the wrath of an offended God. Strangely, that wrath came from the end of a piece of wood—just a stick, a rod that Moses always carried with him—acacia wood, the same kind of tree that burned in the desert.

The rod struck out first at the cobra, Egypt's most powerful protector, and rendered the snake gods harmless by devouring them.

It humiliated the god of the River Nile by turning its muddy waters into blood. The river which was and still is the very life of Egypt became loathsome and foul. It stank and its fish died. The Egyptians were forced to dig for their drinking water. For seven days the muddy river ran red, and a powerful god lost all of his appeal.

As Pharaoh refused to relent, the pressure on Egypt continued. The god Ka, with the body of a man and the head of a frog, was the next victim of the God of Moses.

Teeming hordes of frogs, contrary to their own instincts, swarmed over the land. They covered the broad avenues, hopped into the temples and houses, the kitchens, the ovens, the food, and the beds until all of Egypt was covered with stinking, slimy, croaking frogs.

Frogs leaped up on the throne and emitted their rasping sounds in mockery of Egypt's ruler.

Egyptians again were repulsed by a god they revered. Moses raised his staff against Scarbaeus, the sacred beetle of Egypt—a god of black marble, with a human head attached to a beetle-like body. This god's duty was to protect. Scarbaeus was responsible for keeping the land free from vermin and insects such as lice and fleas.

The dust of the ground was covered with lice. Lice covered the people and plagued the animals. Not a single offering to any of Egypt's multiple gods could be offered since the insects rendered the priests, the temples, and all their sacrifices unclean.

Lice were everywhere, on everything, on everyone—

except in Goshen, where the sons of Israel lived.

The god Apis was the sacred bull-calf of Egypt. Because cattle were sacred and even mummified at death, the Hebrews were unable to make their sacrifices unto God.

It was Apis—the sacred bull-calf, that was shaped by the Hebrews at the base of Mount Sinai.

It was Apis—the sacred cow of the land of mystery—that was dishonored when Moses raised his staff the fifth time.

The land was polluted with the bloated carcasses of thousands of animals—

except in Goshen where the sons of Israel lived.

Amenhotep was furious,

frustrated,
helpless,

but not repentant.

Again the staff was raised. Moses took the ashes of a human sacrifice that the pharaoh had offered to stop the plagues. He sprinkled them into the air.

Another plague followed. Every man, every woman, every child was covered with festering, painful, infectious boils.

The people winced in pain with every movement. The children screamed for relief.

The king secluded himself in agony.

An entire nation came to a complete standstill as its total population was stricken—

except in Goshen where the sons of Israel lived.

The plagues moved from the river to the land, to the animals, to the people, to the skies.

Thunder crashed; fire flashed across the skies as the land of perpetual sunshine was blanketed with hail. The hailstones were so large that they ripped through the crops, tore limbs from trees, and smashed through the palm-covered roofs of the houses. The hail killed the people and the animals that had not taken cover—

except in Goshen where the sons of Israel lived.

Amenhotep repented—until the storm was past. He then persisted in his refusal to allow Israel its freedom.

Moses' staff again was raised.

The god Serapis—who protected Egypt from the locusts—was stripped of his power. The air became thick and dark with flying locusts. Like a giant ocean wave, the insects passed over the plains, the cities, the houses, devouring everything that had not been destroyed by the hail.

The threat of famine and death stalked the country—

except in Goshen where the sons of Israel lived.

The power of Aten Re, the god of the sun—a chief god of Egypt—was smitten by Jehovah.

Darkness—thick, black, impenetrable darkness—fell like a curtain over all of Egypt. The land was paralyzed for seventy-two hours . . . a blackout so complete that people could not see each other.

No one dared to leave his home—

except in Goshen where the sons of Israel lived.

Darkness was followed by death as Amun, the god of life, was rendered powerless.

Egypt wailed in inconsolable grief. Every household felt the pain and helplessness of death—even Pharaoh's child was slain.

The first-born of every family died—

except in Goshen where the sons of Israel lived and believed God by placing the blood of an innocent lamb on the posts of the door.

The Egyptians pled with the Hebrews to leave. They actually paid the Hebrews to leave.

The king said, "Go," and then later rallied six hundred of his select chariots to bring them back.

Chariots and charioteers, king and servants died as the Lord buried them beneath the angry waters of the Red Sea.

Moses wrote a special song and dedicated it to Jehovah, then lifted his gnarled and crooked stick high into the air. As he had once led the chariots to victory in another life, he took command of a new nation and began to lead them to the land of their new home.

The grand city of Memphis, with its temples and columns and obelisks and statues and its gods, has long since died. It lies in the shadows of three stark, crumbling pyramids beneath the ever-shifting sands of the yellow desert.

A few pieces of stone, some chunks from fallen columns and a pathetic statue of Rameses the Great, are all that remain of the once proud capital of the land of the gods.

Its magnificent structures have never been found.

Moses died—forty years later. God buried him in the sands of Mount Nebo without a funeral and without benefit of the rite of mummification.

He emerged—filled with energy, full of life—fourteen centuries later, as a delegate to a special conference held on the peak of Mount Hermon in northern Galilee. There at the Transfiguration of Jesus, in full view of some trainees named Peter, James, and John, he was able to look without restriction into the glorious face of the same God, now in human form, who had spoken from a flaming tree in a barren desert fourteen hundred years before (cf. Matthew 17:1-8).

It all began with a firm belief in *the God of second chances*—a belief that turned a loser into a winner—an unbeliever into a friend of God.

Most of the epitaphs of Egypt's kings have long since crumbled to dust with the stones on which they were carved.

God's epitaph, written in honor of a barefoot shepherd, remains forever in the eternal Book of Books.

It reads:

> . . . no prophet has risen in Israel like Moses, whom the Lord knew face to face, for all the signs and wonders which the Lord sent him to perform in the land of Egypt against Pharaoh, all his servants, and all his land, and for all the mighty power and for all the great terror which Moses performed in the sight of all Israel (Deuteronomy 34:10-12).

Forgotten in Egypt. Erased from the minds of all in the Land of the Pharaohs—but remembered forever by the Lord, and by the world who knows him even today as God's good friend. What Moses needed — and what we need in the midst of life's baffling and bewildering experiences, is not an explanation, but a trust in *the God of second chances.*

BIBLIOGRAPHY

Anati, Emmanuel. "Has Mt. Sinai Been Found?" *Biblical Archaelogy Review*, 11 (July/August 1985).

Archer, Gleason L., Jr. *The Book of Job*. Grand Rapids: Baker Book House, 1982.

The Bedouin, People of the Desert. Produced by Palphot Ltd. Printed in the Holy Land. All rights reserved.

Bernstein, Burton. *Sinai, the Great and Terrible Wilderness*. New York: Viking Press, 1979.

Chafer, Lewis, Sperry. *Systematic Theology*, vol. 1. Dallas, Tex.: Dallas Seminary Press, 1947.

Cook, F. C. *The Bible Commentary*. Grand Rapids: Baker Book House, 1953.

Epp, Theodore H. Moses, vols. 1-4. Lincoln, Neb.: Back to the Bible, 1975.

Haag, Michael. *Guide to Cairo, Including the Pyramids and Saqqara*. Great Britain: Pitman Press, 1985.

Ingraham, J. H. *The Pillar of Fire: Or Israel in Bondage*. Boston: Roberts Brothers, 1887.

Kees, Hermann. *Ancient Egypt, a Cultural Topography*. Chicago: The University of Chicago Press, 1961.

Leacroft, Helen and Richard. *The Buildings of Ancient Egypt*. London: Hodder & Stoughton, 1963.

Luxor. The Egyptian Tourist Authority, 1985.

Macaulay, David. *Pyramid*. Boston: Houghton Mifflin Co., 1975.

Macnaughton, Duncan. *A Scheme of Egyptian Chronology*. London: Luzac & Co., 1932.

Mailer, Norman. *Ancient Evenings*. Boston: Warner Books, 1983.

McGrath, Nancy. *Frommer's Dollarwise Guide to Egypt*. New York: Frommer/Pasmantier Publishers, 1984.

"Moses." *National Geographic Magazine*," January 1976.

National Geographic Society. *Everyday Life in Bible Times*. National Geographic Society, 1967.

Packer, J. I. *Knowing God*. Downers Grove, Ill.: InterVarsity Press, 1973.

Pearlman, Moshe. *In the Footsteps of Moses*. Jerusalem: Steimatzky's Agency, 1973.

Politeyan, J. *Biblical Discoveries in Egypt, Palestine and Mesopotamia*. London: Charles J. Thynne, 1921.

Rawlinson, George. *Moses, His Life and Times*. New York: Fleming H. Revell, 1887.

Roberts, David. *Sinai*. Cairo: Palphot Ltd.

Sinai, Egypt. The Egyptian General Authority for the Promotion of Tourism, Cairo.

Smith, Wilbur M. *Egypt in Biblical Prophecy*. Boston: W.A. Wilde Co., 1957.

Spence, H.D.M. *The Pulpit Commentary, Exodus*. New York: Funk & Wagnalls, 1909.

Strong, Augustus Hopkins. *Systematic Theology, a Compendium*. Philadelphia: Judson Press, 1907.

Tozer, A. W. *The Knowledge of the Holy*. New York: Harper & Bros., 1961.

Unger, Merrill F. *The New Unger's Bible Handbook*. Chicago: Moody Press, 1984.

Watterson, Barbara. *The Gods of Ancient Egypt*. New York: Facts on File Publications, 1984.

West, John Anthony. *The Traveler's Key to Ancient Egypt, a Guide to the Sacred Places of Ancient Egypt.* New York: Alfred A. Knopf, 1985.

Whiston, William. *The Life and Works of Flavius Josephus.* Philadelphia: John C. Winston Co.

Witherby, H. Forbes. *Light from the Land of the Sphinx.* London: Pickering & Inglis.